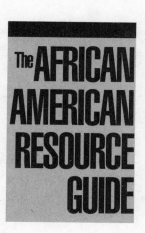

The AFRICAN AMERICAN RESOURCE GUIDE

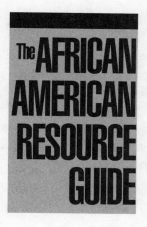

The AFRICAN AMERICAN RESOURCE GUIDE

Anita Doreen Diggs

Barricade Books Inc., New York

Published by Barricade Books Inc.
61 Fourth Avenue
New York, NY 10003

Printed in the United States of America.

Library of Congress Cataloging-in-Publication Data

Diggs, Anita Doreen.
    The African-American resource guide / by Anita Diggs.
        p.   cm.
    ISBN 1-56980-006-5: $12.99
    1. Afro-Americans—Directories. 2. Afro-Americans—
Bibliography. I. Title.
    E185.D45   1994
    016.973'0496073—dc20   93-47551
                                             CIP

Designed by Cindy LaBreacht
First printing

This book is dedicated to my cousin,

ROSCOE GERALD SMITH

(1959-1993) a man of quiet dignity,
strength, and courage.

Acknowledgements

Thanks to Brevard Diggs for years
of encouragement, Mark Jaffe for doing
a wonderful editing/re-organizing job,
Sandy Stuart
for a thorough
and meticulous copyediting job,
and Carole Stuart for her unflagging
interest in my work.

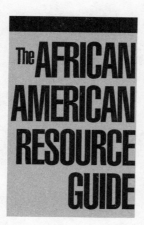

The **AFRICAN AMERICAN RESOURCE GUIDE**

Table of Contents

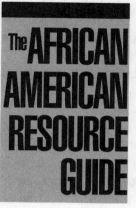

The **AFRICAN AMERICAN RESOURCE GUIDE**

Introduction

"I'd like to network with other blacks in my profession. Are there any organizations that can help me?"

"My child wants to attend a predominantly black college, but the only names I know are Howard and Spelman. Where can I find information about the others?"

"The federal student grant program has been slashed by 50 percent. Are there other sources of financial aid?"

"We're planning a cross-country vacation. Do you have a list of culturally significant places to visit or things to do?"

"My local bookstore does not have many titles by African-Americans. How can I find out about interesting books?"

"Remember Melvin Van Peebles as the fugitive in *Sweet Sweetback's Baadasssss Song*? Is this sexy, revolutionary old film available on videotape?"

THE AFRICAN-AMERICAN RESOURCE GUIDE is intended to answer questions such as these. The guide identifies and describes products and services specifically geared to African-American interests. Individual chapters have been designed as self-contained units, so that the book can be read in its entirety, or particular parts can be consulted as needed.

I've tried to make this reference book as comprehensive and authoritative as possible and would very much appreciate receiving reader feedback, comments, and suggestions for future editions. Please send these to:

Anita Doreen Diggs
c/o Barricade Books Inc.
61 Fourth Avenue
New York, NY 10003

CHAPTER 1

BOOKS

There were few books written by or about African-Americans during the nineteenth century. One exception was *Clotel* by William Wells Brown, an ex-slave who fled to England with the help of a Quaker family. Published in London in 1853, *Clotel* is about a mulatto woman slave who ends her tragic life by drowning in the Potomac River as she is being pursued by a gang of whites. There is much in the novel that condemns President Thomas Jefferson and his views on the subject of slavery. As a result, *Clotel* was not published in the United States until 1867. Even then, the American edition was issued in a revised form in which an anonymous senator is substituted for the president.

White audiences of the period generally turned away from this and other protest novels, preferring the work of Paul Laurence Dunbar who wrote four novels around the turn of the century. Dunbar went out of his way to avoid offending whites and was rewarded with a reputation for literary excellence that endures to this day. A good example of how far Dunbar would go for mainstream acceptance is evident in *The Sport of the Gods* (1902) where he practically urges the black masses to stay down South and provide a labor force for the whites. In this same novel, Dunbar even lamented the wicked influence of northerners on poor and uneducated blacks who wanted to leave the South.

It was not until after the 1960s under the force of the civil rights movement that a significant number of books were published about the anger and discontent in the black community. Never before had so many books appeared about African-Americans as during the decade of the 1960s. Many established mainstream publishers, like McGraw-Hill and Oxford University Press, immediately issued new titles about blacks, and protest novels like *Tell Me How Long The Train's Been Gone* (1968) by James Baldwin became very popular. That was twenty-five years ago. Now, Toni Morrison has become the first African-American ever awarded the Nobel Prize for Literature and, as the following literary resource guide illustrates, African-Americans are now writing on a wide range of subjects and are not limited to apologizing for discontent in the community, protesting racism, or any other single category. The following books are either written by blacks or have an important insight into one or more facets of the black experience that could not be overlooked.

Art and Architecture

BACK OF THE BIG HOUSE: THE ARCHITECTURE OF PLANTATION SLAVERY by John Michael Vlach (University of North Carolina Press; $18.95). This exploration of structures includes more than two-hundred photographs from the Historic American Buildings Survey of the 1930s.

FACE OF THE GODS: ART AND ALTARS OF THE BLACK ATLANTIC WORLD by Robert Farris Thompson (Prestel; $70). This catalog of an exhibition at the Center for African Art in New York shows the impact of African traditions on African-American art.

Autobiography and Biography
ARTS/ENTERTAINMENT

ALL THAT GLITTERED: MY LIFE WITH THE SUPREMES by Tony Turner with Barbaria Aria (Dutton; $19.95). To read this fascinating book is to see the Supremes again in all their glory. Here is Flo Ballard sipping from magnums of Dom Perignon, spreading crackers thick with beluga caviar, and sending crowds wild with her magnificent voice. Here is Diana Ross, driven and powerful, knowing what she wanted and using her intimacy with Berry Gordy as a stepping stone to solo superstardom. Here is Mary Wilson, caught in a circle of friendship and treachery. A riveting account as witnessed by an insider with nothing to hide.

LOUIS ARMSTRONG: AN AMERICAN SUCCESS STORY by James Lincoln Collier (Macmillan; $11.95). This absorbing biography tells Louis Armstrong's story both as a black artist in the United States and as the preeminent jazz artist of all time. Interwoven with the story of his rise to the top is the very real tragedy of his poor musical training and often poor management. Written by one of America's leading authorities on jazz, it is as fascinating as it is informative.

ARSENIO HALL by Norman King (William Morrow and Company; $20). This is the first biography of Arsenio Hall and charts his rise from the mean streets of Cleveland to the glitter of after-hours Hollywood. An interesting look at the man who says "To be successful and a black man in this country, you have to be bicultural."

AS NASTY AS THEY WANNA BE: THE UNCENSORED STORY OF LUTHER CAMPBELL OF THE 2 LIVE CREW by Luther Campbell and John R. Miller (Barricade Books; $17.95). The autobiography of the millionaire rap star whose controversial lyrics landed him in jail and sparked a national debate on rap and the First Amendment.

BROTHER RAY: RAY CHARLES' OWN STORY by Ray Charles and David Ritz (Da Capo Press; $13.95). Ray Charles has overcome poverty, blindness, and the loss of his parents. By combining the influences of gospel, jazz, blues, and country music, he has won worldwide acclaim and enjoyed a career spanning fifty years. The book is as engaging, frank, funny, and soulful as Ray Charles' enduring music.

CALL HER MISS ROSS: THE UNAUTHORIZED BIOGRAPHY OF DIANA ROSS by J. Randy Taraborrelli (Birch Lane Press; $21.95). The author conducted 403 interviews to write this vivid portrait of one of the world's greatest superstars. Here is the story of Diana's romances with Smokey Robinson, Ryan O'Neal, and Berry Gordy. It also explores her troubled relationship with Michael Jackson.

DANCING SPIRIT by Judith Jamison with Howard Kaplan (Doubleday; $25). The life story of the first black superstar of American dance.

DELIVER US FROM TEMPTATION by Tony Turner (Thunder's Mouth Press; $22.95). The story of the rise and tragic fall of the Temptations by the group's former road manager.

ELLA FITZGERALD: FIRST LADY OF AMERICAN SONG by Bud Kliment (Melrose Square; $3.95). This beautifully told biography traces Ella Fitzgerald's fascinating life from her birth in Virginia to the White House and international acclaim as America's "First Lady of Song."

JOSEPHINE: THE HUNGRY HEART by Jean-Claude Baker and Chris Chase (Random House; $25). This is an oral history of the life and times of the great entertainer who took Paris by storm as seen through the eyes of her adopted son.

LATOYA: GROWING UP IN THE JACKSON FAMILY by LaToya Jackson with Patricia Romanowski (Dutton; $19.95). Jackson reveals the disastrous cost of the most dazzling success story in American show business.

MICHAEL JACKSON: THE MAGIC & THE MADNESS by J. Randy Taraborrelli (Carol Publishing; $21.95). Examines the amazing career and tumultuous private life of the world's most enigmatic performer.

MURPHY by Dennis P. Eichhorn (Turman Publishing Company; $3.25). Eddie Murphy's story from the first time he performed onstage in 1976 to his roles on "Saturday Night Live."

RICHARD PRYOR: THE MAN BEHIND THE LAUGHTER by Joseph Nazel (Holloway House; $2.50). Richard Pryor's life story reads like a work of exciting, if improbable, fiction. It begins in Peoria, Illinois, where his mother was a prostitute in his grandmother's bordello, and it follows his journey from the streets to show business. Once a success, Pryor struggled with addiction to cocaine and other drugs and a near brush with death after being burned in a mysterious fire in his home.

SMOKEY: INSIDE MY LIFE by Smokey Robinson (McGraw Hill; $18.95). In this candid and powerful book, Smokey Robinson writes of the peaks and valleys of his life and career. He describes his friendships and encounters with such superstars as Diana Ross, Michael Jackson, Aretha Franklin, Marvin Gaye, Stevie Wonder, and legendary Motown boss Berry Gordy. He tells of the tragedy of losing his mother at age ten and discusses his complicated relationship with his father. With remarkable frankness, Robinson talks about the extramarital affairs that cost him his marriage and reveals how his deadly addiction to cocaine almost destroyed his career and his life.

TRIUMPH & TRAGEDY: THE TRUE STORY OF THE SUPREMES by Marianne Ruuth (Holloway House; $2.95). Marianne Ruuth interviewed former members of the Supremes, friends, and associates for an in depth look at those three young women with whom all of America fell in love back in the 1960s.

BUSINESS/ENTERPRISE

BEYOND THE TIMBERLINE: THE TRIALS AND TRIUMPHS OF A BLACK ENTREPRENEUR by T. M. Alexander, Sr. (M. E. Duncan & Co; $21.95). An Atlanta insurance and real estate tycoon offers witty anecdotes and slogans on hard work and success. Alexander tells how he overcame southern racial barriers to build a multimillion-dollar empire.

MADAM C. J. WALKER by Cookie Lommel (Holloway House; $3.95). Story of the black business executive who created a line of beauty products, developed a chain of salons, and started the sales-agent party plan system, now used by Mary Kay. When Madam C. J. Walker died in 1919, she was America's first black female millionaire.

SUCCEEDING AGAINST THE ODDS by John H. Johnson (Amistad; $12.95). The autobiography of the publisher of *Ebony* and *Jet* magazines who rose from the welfare rolls of the Depression to become one of the most successful black businessmen in American history.

CIVIL RIGHTS/POLITICS

THE AUTOBIOGRAPHY OF MALCOLM X edited by Alex Haley (Ballantine; $5.95). The absorbing personal story of the man who rose from a life of crime to become the most dynamic leader of the black revolution. This book shows the man behind the stereotyped image of the hate preacher to reveal a sensitive, proud, highly intelligent person who knew he would not live long enough to see this book in print.

DOWN THE LINE: THE COLLECTED WRITINGS OF BAYARD RUSTIN (Quadrangle Books; $10). The product of an activist who is also a theoretician, a political organizer who is also a serious writer, Rustin's essays and articles provide a clear, balanced, and deeply moving history of the struggle for civil rights in America.

DREAM MAKERS, DREAM BREAKERS: THE WORLD OF JUSTICE THURGOOD MARSHALL by Carl T. Rowan (Little, Brown and Co.; $24.95). A biography of one of the towering figures of the American judicial system. Journalist Carl T. Rowan draws upon forty years of friendship and hours of interviews to write a detailed account of the first black Supreme Court justice's incredible life.

FLY IN THE BUTTERMILK: THE LIFE STORY OF CECIL REED by Cecil A. Reed with Priscilla Donovan (University of Iowa Press; $29.95). The autobiography of an African-American man who lived and prospered in all-white midwestern communities.

JESSE JACKSON by Eddie Stone (Holloway House; $3.95). One of the country's most popular black leaders, Jesse Jackson is not without his critics. To many he is just too flamboyant. Others find his political ideas somewhat vague. Nevertheless he has proven he can pull in the votes whether in Vermont, Mississippi, or Michigan.

JESSE JACKSON AND POLITICAL POWER by Teresa Celsi (Millbrook Press; $4.95). The story of Jesse Jackson from his humble beginnings in Greenville, South Carolina, to his activities during the 1988 presidential election year.

STANDING FAST: THE AUTOBIOGRAPHY OF ROY WILKINS (Viking; $16.95). The stories of Roy Wilkin's life and the modern civil rights movement are inextricably linked. A relentless pragmatist, who advocated change through legal action, Wilkins participated in virtually every major civil rights advance and will go down in history as one of the great leaders of the century. He worked for the integration of the army, helped to plan and organize the historic march on Washington, and pushed presidents from FDR to Carter to implement civil rights legislation.

KING OF THE CATS: THE LIFE AND TIMES OF ADAM CLAYTON POWELL, JR. by Wil Haygood (Houghton Mifflin; $24.95). Chronicles the public and private life of the first black congressman from Harlem. The mercurial politician shunned partisan conventions yet labored tirelessly within the political system to enact laws benefiting the poor.

THURGOOD MARSHALL: WARRIOR AT THE BAR, REBEL ON THE BENCH by Michael D. Davis and Hunter R. Clark (Birch Lane Press; $24.95). A biography of the first black Supreme Court justice and NAACP lawyer who helped win the landmark *Brown* v. *Board of Education* case that outlawed segregation in public schools.

PUSHED BACK TO STRENGTH: A BLACK WOMAN'S JOURNEY HOME by Gloria Wade-Gayles, foreword by Johnnetta Cole (Beacon Press; $20). Traces Wade-Gayles' life from a southern housing project through her civil rights movement activism to academia.

SOLEDAD BROTHER: THE PRISON LETTERS OF GEORGE JACKSON (Bantam; $2.95). On August 21, 1971, two days before the opening of his murder trial, George Jackson was killed inside San Quentin prison. The authorities say that he was shot while trying to escape. His letters to his mother, father, brother, and Angela Davis survived, and through these letters, Jackson became a symbol for the struggle of all oppressed people. This collection of his correspondence reveals his extraordinary courage and passion.

SOJOURNER TRUTH by Peter Krass (Holloway House; $3.95). An electrifying public speaker, Sojourner Truth was a leader in the crusade against slavery in mid-nineteenth century America. Born into slavery in 1797, she was auctioned off as a child to another slaveowner and separated from her family. She was finally given her freedom in 1827 and was soon renowned throughout the East for her eloquence and wisdom. Her reputation spread even further in 1850 when she published the story of her life as a slave. She then embarked on wide-ranging lecture tours to advocate the end of slavery and the need for women's rights.

A TASTE OF POWER: A BLACK WOMAN'S STORY by Elaine Brown (Pantheon Books; $25). Elaine Brown's account of her life at the highest levels of the Black Panthers' hierarchy illuminates more than the pain of sexism and the struggle behind racism. It is also the story of Elaine's relationship with Huey Newton, a brilliant yet complex man who became Elaine's lover and ultimately her nemesis.

HARRIET TUBMAN: THE MOSES OF HER PEOPLE by Sarah Bradford (Applewood Books; $8.95). This book was originally published in 1869 and is a classic biography of the black woman who defied the law and bounty hunters to lead dozens of her people out of slavery.

NAT TURNER: PROPHET AND SLAVE LEADER

by Terry Bisson (Melrose Square; $3.95). Fiery preacher, militant leader, and prophet, Nat Turner organized a slave uprising that struck a defiant blow against slavery in the United States thirty years before the Civil War.

UP FROM SLAVERY by Booker T. Washington (Penguin

Classics; $4.95). During his unchallenged reign as black America's foremost spokesman, former slave Booker T. Washington treaded a dangerous middle ground in a time of racial backlash and disfranchisement. This book reveals the conviction he held that the black man's salvation lay in education, industriousness and self reliance.

W.E.B. DU BOIS: 1868-1919, BIOGRAPHY OF A RACE

by David Levering Lewis (Henry Holt; $35). The story of William Edward Burghart Du Bois, the scholar, writer, and founder of the NAACP.

FAMILY

DUKE ELLINGTON IN PERSON: AN INTIMATE

MEMOIR (Da Capo; $14.95) by Mercer Ellington with Stanley Dance. In this unique memoir, Mercer Ellington unflinchingly reveals the amorous entanglements, superstitions, musical competitiveness, disdain of formal training, and business and social cunning behind his father's persona. There are also abundant insights into Ellington's musical genius which produced such immortal classics as "Take The A Train," "Satin Doll," "Sophisticated Lady," and "Mood

Indigo." Few accounts recreate so vividly the teeming jazz life of Washington D.C. in the twenties and Harlem of the thirties and forties.

LOVE IN BLACK AND WHITE by Mark and Gail Mathabane (HarperCollins; $20). The odyssey of an American interracial couple and how they have dealt with opposition from family members and society at large.

MAGGIE'S AMERICAN DREAM: THE LIFE AND TIMES OF A BLACK FAMILY by James P. Comer, M.D. (NAL Books; $18.95). A doctor looks back on his mother's life and her dream that all her children would become college graduates.

MOM & POP WINANS: STORIES FROM HOME (FMG Books; $8.95) is the autobiography of one of the most celebrated and prolific musical families currently on the gospel and popular music charts. In nearly forty years of marriage, David and Delores Winans not only produced 10 children— David, Ronald, Calvin, Marvin, Michael, Daniel, BeBe, CeCe, Angie, and Debbie—they gave birth to a musical dynasty that has brought legions of new fans to gospel music. In their jointly composed autobiography, coauthored by Lisa T. Groswiler, the elder Winans trace the family's climb and discuss the legacy of music and faith that they have attempted to pass on to their children and grandchildren.

PRIDE OF FAMILY: FOUR GENERATIONS OF AMERICAN WOMEN OF COLOR by Carole Ione (Avon Books; $10) recalls the ambition and spirit of the author's ancestors, who include a vaudeville dancer and one of the first black women doctors in Washington D.C.

QUEEN by Alex Haley and David Stevens (William Morrow & Company; $25.00). This multi-generational saga focuses on Haley's grandmother, Queen. It traces Haley's great-great-grandfather James Jackson, Sr., from Ireland to Nashville to Alabama, where he establishes his plantation Forks of Cypress Hills. Jackson's son Jass inherits the plantation on the eve of the Civil War. He falls passionately in love with a strong willed slave named Easter and together they have a daughter—Queen.

ROOTS by Alex Haley (Dell $6.99). The story of the Haley clan from the enslavement of a Mandinka warrior, Kunta Kunte, to the birth of the author. This book is the story of all African-Americans and should be required reading for everyone in the black community.

SOUL TO SOUL: A BLACK RUSSIAN AMERICAN FAMILY 1865-1992 by Yalena Khanga with Susan Jacoby (W.W. Norton; $22.95). Autobiography of the young Russian granddaughter of two American communist emigres to the Soviet Union—one black, one white. She tells her family's saga through four generations beginning with racial oppression in late nineteenth century Mississippi.

SWEET SUMMER: GROWING UP WITH AND WITHOUT MY DAD by Bebe Moore Campbell (Putnam; $18.95). Summers were when Bebe Moore Campbell grew close to her father. That was the season when his fast car raced from Philadelphia to the Tidewater region of North Carolina with his prized daddy's girl. From the heat of those summers emerges this powerful memoir of the bond between a daughter and a father who were separated by divorce.

HISTORICAL

THE DUKE ELLINGTON READER edited by Mark Tucker (Oxford University Press; $30). This first historical anthology of writings about Ellington's life and music is a treasure chest of some one hundred essays and remembrances by such authors as Ralph Ellison, Gunther Schuller, Stanley Crouch, Nat Hentoff, Albert Murray, and Stanley Dance.

DU BOIS: A PICTORIAL BIOGRAPHY by Shirley Graham Du Bois (Johnson Publishing Co; $14.95). The life of W. E. B. Du Bois is recalled through these photographs. This volume traces his life from his infancy to the days shortly before his death in Accra, Ghana.

PAUL ROBESON: ATHLETE, ACTOR, SINGER, ACTIVIST by Scott Ehrlich (Melrose Square; $3.95). This is the story of the gifted man who went from All-American football player at Rutgers (where he was graduated first in his class) to win worldwide respect as a performer.

HARRIET TUBMAN: CALL TO FREEDOM by Judy Carlson (Fawcett Columbine; $3.95). Imagine running for your life through a dark forest, knowing that if you are caught by your pursuers, you face a fate worse than death. In the 1850s Harriet Tubman lived through this frightening experience not once but eighteen times as she helped other black slaves find their way to freedom in the North.

WHOLE WORLD IN HIS HANDS: A PICTORIAL BIO OF PAUL ROBESON by Susan Robeson (Citadel Press; $14.95). An illustrated look at the life of the great actor, activist, and orator.

JOURNALISM

BLACK IS THE COLOR OF MY TV TUBE by Gil Noble (Lyle Stuart; $9.95). The author is an award-winning TV newsman who recounts his experiences as a black man in the world of broadcasting.

BREAKING BARRIERS by Carl T. Rowan (Little Brown and Company; $22.95). Rowan is an award-winning syndicated columnist and host of his own radio show. In this hard hitting memoir, he unfolds the fascinating story of how he rose from abject poverty in McMinnville, Tennessee, to a life at the forefront of power and social change.

IN MY PLACE by Charlayne Hunter Gault (Farrar, Straus, Giroux; $19). Memoirs of the celebrated journalist who was one of the first two black students admitted to the University of Georgia in 1961. The book traces the fire bombings and riots that followed her enrollment at the all white college and her illustrious career as a magazine, newspaper, and television journalist.

LITERARY

BLACK BOY by Richard Wright (HarperPerennial; $6.00). In this once sensational, now classic autobiography, Richard Wright tells with unforgettable fury and eloquence what he felt as a "black boy" in the Jim Crow South.

THE FIRE NEXT TIME by James Baldwin (Vintage; $8). A powerful evocation of his early life in Harlem and a disturbing examination of the consequences of racial injustice. This book galvanized the nation in the early days of the civil rights movement and stands as one of black America's most essential works.

FROM SLAVE DAYS TO THE PRESENT: 25 AFRICAN-AMERICANS REVEAL THE TRIALS AND TRIUMPHS OF THEIR CHILDHOODS (Avon; $9). Essays by Malcolm X, Maya Angelou, Booker T. Washington, and others.

I KNOW WHY THE CAGED BIRD SINGS by Maya Angelou (Bantam; $3.95). The story of the author's early years in a small rural community. A beautiful book which reveals the courage, dignity, and endurance of a young girl.

KAFFIR BOY IN AMERICA by Mark Mathabane (Collier Books; $10). A South African boy escapes to America and recounts his coming of age in a country overwhelming in its size, wealth, poverty, and despair.

MANCHILD IN THE PROMISED LAND by Claude Brown (Signet; $5.99). Claude Brown is a black man who made it out of the ghetto gang wars, crime, and drugs to become a law student at one of America's leading universities. It is one of the most extraordinary autobiographies of our time.

ORDER OUT OF CHAOS: THE AUTOBIOGRAPHICAL WORKS OF MAYA ANGELOU (Virago Press; $13.95). A critical examination of the life and work of the acclaimed writer/performer edited by Dolly A. McPherson, literary executor of the Maya Angelou Papers, which are housed in the Z. Smith Reynolds library at Wake Forest University.

A SMALL PLACE by Jamaica Kincaid (Plume; $6.95). In this expansive essay, the author gives us a view of Antigua that vacationers never think of which include the history of its people, their manners, sense of time, and opinions of the tourists who stare at them.

TO BE YOUNG, GIFTED AND BLACK by Lorraine Hansberry (Signet; $4.95). The story of the famous writer who was born in Chicago, moved to New York, and won fame with her first play. She went on to new heights of artistry before her tragically early death.

SPORTS

ARTHUR ASHE: PORTRAIT IN MOTION by Arthur Ashe with Frank Deford (Carroll & Graf; $11.95). A look at a year in the life of a sports superstar based on a diary he kept between the 1974 and 1975 Wimbledon tournaments.

I HAD A HAMMER: THE HANK AARON STORY by Hank Aaron with Lonnie Wheeler (HarperPaperbacks; $5.50). In thrilling, high-charged fashion, Aaron tells all about his family life and friendships, clubhouse hijinks plus on-field thrills and the difficulties of being black in baseball.

JORDAN by Dennis P. Eichhorn (Turman Publishing Company; $3.25). The story of Michael Jordan, the phenomenal guard who played for the Chicago Bulls of the National Basketball Association, from his birth in Brooklyn, New York, to sports superstardom.

MAGIC by Michael Morgan (Turman Publishing Company; $3.25). Magic Johnson's story from his childhood in Lansing, Michigan, where he was bused to high school to achieve racial integration to his days as a basketball player for the Los Angeles Lakers.

MUHAMMAD ALI: A VIEW FROM THE CORNER by Ferdie Pacheco (Birch Lane Press; $21.95). Pacheco provides a fresh, revealing view of Ali's family, friends, and lovers. The book is peppered throughout with on-the-scene sketches and rare photographs from the author's personal collection.

MY LIFE by Earvin "Magic" Johnson with William Novak (Random House; $22). The basketball star gives an intimate account of his family and friends, his acclaimed basketball career, and his fight against the virus that causes AIDS.

JACKIE ROBINSON: FIRST BLACK IN PROFESSIONAL BASEBALL by Richard Scott (Melrose Square; $3.95). The story of the man who was good enough, professional enough, and most of all, man enough to be selected to break the "color barrier" in professional baseball.

Beauty

COLOR TO COLOR: THE BLACK WOMAN'S GUIDE TO A RAINBOW OF FASHION AND BEAUTY by Jean E. Patton (Fireside Books; $13). A professional image consultant solves fashion and image problems for women from all walks of life by showing how to select and work with colors, fabrics, cosmetics, and styles.

Business and Personal Finance

BLACK LIFE IN CORPORATE AMERICA: SWIMMING IN THE MAINSTREAM by George Davis and Glegg Watson (Anchor Press; $14.95). A look at the professional and personal lives of black men and women trying to make it in a world created by and for white males. Confronted by rules, protocol, habits, manners, values, and styles of thinking that are not their own, these men and women tell the deeply moving story of their struggles to find a home in foreign social space.

THE BLACK MANAGER by Floyd Dickens, Jr. and Jacqueline B. Dickens (Amacon; $22.95). Based on a study of successful black managers, this book reveals how blacks can nurture the attitudes and skills necessary to excel in the workplace and still maintain their personal values.

CHILDREN OF THE DREAM: THE PSYCHOLOGY OF BLACK SUCCESS by Audrey Edwards and Dr. Craig K. Polite (Doubleday; $21.50). The authors define black success in the last thirty years as the realization of an American promise—access to equal opportunity. For more than two years, they traveled the country seeking out those black men and women who have achieved positions of power and influence in the American workplace. The one common trait presented here is that successful blacks are empowered by a positive sense of racial identity.

THE MINORITY CAREER GUIDE by Michael Kastre, Nydia Rodriguez Kastre, and Al Edwards (Peterson's Guides; $11.95). What affirmative action and the EEO can and can't do, strategies for handling illegal interview questions, how to build a strong career, and more.

SUCCESS AT WORK: A GUIDE FOR AFRICAN-AMERICANS by Anita Doreen Diggs (Barricade Books; $12.99). A savvy view of how to handle the race factor while climbing the ladder from entry-level jobs to middle management. Topics include: getting along with the boss; handling difficult co-workers; dealing with the office Tom; entertaining whites at home; and how to break out of corporate life. Speaks not only to the young college graduate entering the job market for the first time, but also to African-Americans who are already working in corporate America and wondering why they aren't moving up.

WORK SISTER WORK: WHY BLACK WOMEN CAN'T GET AHEAD AND WHAT THEY CAN DO ABOUT IT by Cydney Shields and Leslie C. Shields (Birch Lane Press; $19.95). This book is directed to the black woman who wants to take control of her life and achieve career satisfaction. Checklists, charts, and self-quizzes point the way to improvement, and helpful hints, tips, and survival techniques show the black working woman how to get from where she is to where she wants to go. More than a how-to guide, it is intimate and inspirational.

Child Care and Parenting

AFRICAN NAMES: NAMES FROM THE AFRICAN CONTINENT FOR CHILDREN AND ADULTS by Julia Stewart (Citadel Press; $9.95). From Aba to Zuri, this book offers more than 1,000 names from all corners of the African continent—as well as 175 surnames—for adults of African descent to name their children or to substitute for their own western names. The book also includes tidbits of information about African geography, history, linguistics, culture, and rulers.

BLACK FATHERHOOD: THE GUIDE TO MALE PARENTING by Earl Ofari Hutchinson, Ph.D. (Middle Passage Press; $8.95). This national bestseller explodes the stereotypes about black men as fathers by focusing on fathers that enrich their families. It is not a book about defeatism and despair but one that tells the story of what some black men are doing right.

RAISING BLACK CHILDREN by Dr. Alvin F. Poussaint and Dr. James P. Comer (Plume; $12). Two doctors respond to hundreds of commonly asked questions about black children's development from infancy to adolescence. Additionally, Poussaint and Comer tackle more complex problems, such as building self-esteem in black children in the face of race prejudice.

Civil Rights Movement

EYES ON THE PRIZE: AMERICA'S CIVIL RIGHTS YEARS 1954-1965 by Juan Williams, Penguin Introduction by Julian Bond (Penguin; $10.95). This book brings America's civil rights years to life. Here are the heroes and heroines, the brilliant strategies, the national politics, the violence. Here, too, are the white segregationists who defended the old ways as "southern tradition." From leaders like Martin Luther King, Jr., to teenager Barbara Rose Johns, *Eyes on the Prize* captures the sweep of the movement.

FREEDOM BOUND: A HISTORY OF AMERICA'S CIVIL RIGHTS MOVEMENT by Robert Weisbrot (Plume; $11). The full story of the civil rights movement from its rise with the Brown decision and the Montgomery bus boycott in the 1950s, through the dramatic sit-ins, freedom rides, marches, and great legislative achievements of the 1960s, to its decline in the urban riots and disputes over community control and affirmative action in the late 1960s and 1970s. Weisbrot argues that the movement foundered when it shifted course from political to social goals.

LET FREEDOM RING: A DOCUMENTARY HISTORY OF THE MODERN CIVIL RIGHTS MOVEMENT by Peter B. Levy (Praeger; $15.95). Traces the story of the civil rights movement through the words of those who participated in it.

MALCOLM X: THE MAN AND HIS TIME edited by John Henrik Clarke (Africa World Press; $14.95). Malcolm X's central role in the black liberation movement emerges vividly in his own words. Issues such as his deep involvement in Islam and his influence on the political consciousness of African-Americans are explored.

PARTING THE WATERS: AMERICA IN THE KING YEARS 1954-1963 by Taylor Branch (Touchstone/Simon & Schuster; $14.95). A story of the civil rights movement from the fiery political baptism of Martin Luther King, Jr., to the corridors of Camelot where the Kennedy brothers weighed the demands for justice against the deceptions of J. Edgar Hoover.

**THE SUMMER THAT DIDN'T END: THE STORY OF
THE MISSISSIPPI CIVIL RIGHTS PROJECT OF 1964**
by Len Holt, Preface by Julian Bond (Da Capo Press;
$14.95). During the summer of 1964, America suddenly
lost its innocence. By October, as a terrible by-product of
the Freedom Summer Project in Mississippi, there had been
fifteen murders—including those of the three young civil-
rights workers in Neshoba County. This book was the first
to tell the full story of the Mississippi civil rights project. Len
Holt set out to answer the questions evoked by the killings:
Why did the federal government offer no protection to the
freedom workers? What, indeed, was the role of the federal
government in the South? And why did the FBI refuse to aid
the investigation until it was too late?

VOICES OF FREEDOM by Henry Hampton and Steven
Fayer (Bantam; $15.95). An oral history of the civil rights
movement from the 1950s through the 1980s. In this
monumental volume, Henry Hampton, creator and executive
producer of the acclaimed PBS series "Eyes On The Prize,"
and Steven Fayer, series writer, draw upon nearly one
thousand interviews with civil rights activists, politicians,
reporters, Justice Department officials, and hundreds of
ordinary people who took part in the struggle, weaving a
fascinating narrative of the civil rights movement told by the
people who lived it.

Civil War and Reconstruction

BLACK RECONSTRUCTION IN AMERICA by W. E. B.
Du Bois (Atheneum; $18). Originally published in 1935, this
was the first full length study of the role African-Americans
played in the crucial period after the American Civil War.

THOMAS MORRIS CHESTER, BLACK CIVIL WAR CORRESPONDENT: HIS DISPATCHES FROM THE VIRGINIA FRONT edited by R. J. M. Blackett (Da Capo; $13.95). The only black correspondent for a major daily newspaper during the Civil War, Chester covered the crucial final year of the war around Richmond. His dispatches constitute the most sustained and extensive firsthand account of black soldiers in existence. As the war came to a close, Chester richly described the responses of Confederate troops and civilians to encounters with black soldiers, as he joined the black troops of the twenty-fifth Army Corps as they led the victorious Union forces into Richmond.

Contemporary Affairs

AMERICAN ODYSSEY: HAITIANS IN NEW YORK CITY by Michel S. Laguerre (Cornell University Press; $14.95). An assessment of the economic and social growth of the Haitian immigrant community in New York City.

CLIMBING JACOB'S LADDER: THE FUTURE OF AFRICAN-AMERICAN FAMILIES by Andrew Billingsley, with a foreword by Paula Giddings (Simon & Schuster; $27.50). An in-depth examination of the effects of history, technology, education, politics, and the economy on the African-American family.

DEADLY CONSEQUENCES: HOW VIOLENCE IS DESTROYING OUR TEENAGE POPULATION AND A PLAN TO BEGIN SOLVING THE PROBLEM by Deborah Prothrow-Stith, M.D. with Michaele Veissman (HarperPerennial; $12). A comprehensive analysis of the endemic violence ravaging a generation of young people.

DEALS WITH THE DEVIL by Pearl Cleage (One World/Ballantine; $22). A playwright/performance artist/essayist offers her perspective on male-female relationships, politics, culture, and survival in the African-American community.

MAMA MIGHT BE BETTER OFF DEAD: THE FAILURE OF HEALTH CARE IN URBAN AMERICA by Laurie Kaye Abraham (University of Chicago Press; $22.50). A health care reporter chronicles the real health care problems of four generations in a poor African-American family.

UPON THIS ROCK: THE MIRACLES OF A BLACK CHURCH by Samuel G. Freedman (HarperCollins; $22.50). A profile of Johnny Ray Youngblood, the pastor of a church that thrives in one of the nation's most desperate slums.

WE HAVE A DREAM: AFRICAN-AMERICAN VISIONS OF FREEDOM edited by Diana Wells (Carroll & Graf; $11.95). The legacy of Martin Luther King, Jr., as expressed in brilliant heartfelt essays by Alex Haley, Malcolm X, and many others.

Cookbooks, Wine and Entertainment

THE AFRICAN COOKBOOK by Bea Sandler (Citadel Press; $12.95). In her travels, the late Bea Sandler learned about African eating customs and food preparation methods. She compiled menus for complete meals from eleven African countries—Senegal, the Sudan, Mozambique, Madagascar, Ethiopia, Kenya, Liberia, South Africa, Morocco, Ghana, and Tanzania. Sandler devotes a chapter to each country, describing its culinary customs and giving suggestions on how anyone can prepare a complete and authentic African dinner.

THE BLACK FAMILY REUNION COOKBOOK by the National Council of Negro Women (Simon & Schuster/Fireside Books; $12). The book combines "food memories" with recipes by Dionne Warwick, Patti LaBelle, Maxine Waters, and others.

JUMPING THE BROOM: THE AFRICAN-AMERICAN WEDDING PLANNER by Harriette Cole (Holt; $27.50). The fashion editor of *Essence* suggests ways to incorporate Afrocentric customs into the traditional celebration.

SYLVIA'S SOUL FOOD: RECIPES FROM HARLEM'S WORLD FAMOUS RESTAURANT by Sylvia Woods and Christopher Styler (Hearst Books; $17). Sylvia Woods has been barbecuing, baking, frying, and smothering food in her New York restaurant for nearly thirty years. In this book she reveals more than one hundred of her recipe secrets.

TASTING BRAZIL: REGIONAL RECIPES AND REMINISCENCES by Jessica B. Harris (Macmillan; $23). Combines 125 Brazilian recipes with cultural history and travel reminiscences.

Culture and Sociology

THE AFRICAN-AMERICAN HOLIDAY OF KWANZAA: A CELEBRATION OF FAMILY, COMMUNITY AND CULTURE by Maulana Karenga (University of Sankore Press, $5.95). The creator of Kwanzaa discusses the origin, meaning, and activities of the celebration.

BLACK RAGE by William H. Grier and Price M. Cobbs (Basic Books; $13). The first book to examine the full range of black life from the vantage point of psychiatry, this widely acclaimed work has established itself as the classic statement of the desperation, conflicts, and anger of black life in America today. It tells of the psychic stresses engendered by discrimination and focuses on the miasma of racial hatred in America, why it exists, and what will surely happen if it is not soon dispelled.

BLACK STUDIES, RAP AND THE ACADEMY by Houston A. Baker, Jr. (University of Chicago Press; $14.95). A discussion of the cultural importance of rap and its role as a new form of urban expression. Houston Baker offers a vigorous commentary on the cultural importance of rap and a passionate argument for the responsibility of intellectuals to this newest form of urban expression.

BROKEN SILENCES: INTERVIEWS WITH BLACK AND WHITE WOMEN WRITERS edited by Shirley M. Jordan (Rutgers University Press; $22.95). In these twenty interviews with women writers of fiction, Jordan—a professor at Hampton University—attempts to plumb the relations between black and white women in fiction and in life and to explore the creative process.

ELEVATING THE GAME: THE HISTORY AND AESTHETICS OF BLACK MEN IN BASKETBALL by Nelson George (Simon & Schuster; $11). A historical look at how African-American male athletes have transformed the game of basketball and how their presence has affected race relations and perceptions of black men in America.

THE FLIP SIDE OF SOUL by Bob Teague (William Morrow & Company; $15.95). Bob Teague has been a distinguished award winning journalist at NBC for more than twenty-five years, making him one of the deans of TV newscasting. Here, in a series of letters to his son Adam, he talks about the status of today's black Americans. Teague says the time has come for black men and women to set high standards for themselves. He urges strong families and parental responsibilities as a way out of the welfare quagmire. Teague's is a powerful message, important to all Americans.

GERRI MAJOR'S BLACK SOCIETY by Geraldyn Hodges Major with Doris E. Saunders (Johnson Publishing Co., $25). This provocative and insightful book answers the many questions which revolve around the many aspects of "black society." Written by a woman who has spent half a century chronicling the activities of this largely unknown class of Americans.

NOBODY KNOWS MY NAME by James Baldwin (Vintage; $10). A collection of illuminating, deeply felt essays on topics ranging from race relations to the role of the writer in society.

THE PRICE OF THE TICKET: COLLECTED NONFICTION OF JAMES BALDWIN 1948-1985 (St. Martin's Press; $29.95). James Baldwin was one of the major American voices of this century. Nowhere is this more evident than in this book which includes every important piece of nonfiction that Baldwin ever wrote. It combines the intensely private experience with a deep examination of black-white relations. The work is at once an autobiography and an exploration of the twentieth century black intellectual experience.

WHY BLACK PEOPLE TEND TO SHOUT by Ralph Wiley (Carol Publishing; $15.95). The author takes on popular culture as it relates to black Americans today. His scope includes everyone from Marion Barry and Nietzsche to Bernhard Goetz, Jackie Robinson, Spike Lee, and H. L. Mencken cutting to the heart of issues that continue to tear people apart.

WHY I LEFT AMERICA AND OTHER ESSAYS by Oliver W. Harrington (University Press of Mississippi; $20). A gifted African-American artist talks about his country, the culture that produced him, and what made him finally leave it.

Drama

THE AMEN CORNER by James Baldwin (Dell; $5.99). Baldwin uses razor sharp dialogue to peel away the public image of charismatic preacher Sister Margaret and reveal a wounded woman's heart. Baldwin once again lets us witness the dilemma of the black man who desires what the world has stolen—his manhood and his dreams.

BLACK DRAMA ANTHOLOGY edited by Woodie King and Ron Miller (New American Library; $6.95). Twenty-three plays from contemporary playwrights including Imamu Amiri Baraka, Joseph Walker, and Archie Schepp.

THE MOTION OF HISTORY AND OTHER PLAYS by Amiri Baraka (William Morrow and Company; $8.95). A volume of three plays in which Baraka explores the nature of white, capitalist society.

9 PLAYS BY BLACK WOMEN edited by Margaret B. Wilkerson (Mentor; $5.95). Whether it is the brilliant fragment of Lorraine Hansberry's unfinished historical drama or Aishah Rahman's compelling underground classic of teenage pregnancy, these plays speak persuasively from the particular vantage point of black women. The result is extraordinary drama.

Fiction

AFTER THE GARDEN by Doris Jean Austin (NAL Books; $17.95). Jersey City is the setting of this novel about a beautiful, sheltered young girl named Elzina Tompkins who searches for happiness and fulfillment in the 1940s and fifties. A wonderful cast of characters whose individuality and strength give them a special, tough beauty.

AND DO REMEMBER ME by Marita Golden (Doubleday; $19). A historical novel set during the freedom summer of 1964 that depicts the friendship of two women caught in the frenzy of great social upheaval.

BELOVED by Toni Morrison (Plume; $9.95). Winner of the 1988 Pulitzer Prize. A story set in the times of slavery and a woman who kills her own child to set it free.

BLACK VOICES edited by Abraham Chapman (Mentor; $5.99). In this exciting and varied anthology, Professor Chapman has brought together many of the writers who reflect the enormous artistic vitality of the black community. Here are the works of world famous figures as well as lesser known authors. This is a sampling of some of the finest talents this country has produced.

BREAKING ICE: AN ANTHOLOGY OF CONTEMPORARY AFRICAN-AMERICAN FICTION edited by Terry McMillan (Penguin Books; $14). Here are fifty-seven short stories by a fine collection of African-American writers with strong voices, viewpoints, and very real talent.

BROWN GIRL, BROWNSTONES by Paule Marshall (The Feminist Press; $8.95). Set in Brooklyn during the Depression and World War II, this is the fiercely told story of Barbadian immigrants striving to surmount poverty and racism and make their new country home.

CAMBRIDGE by Caryl Phillips (Knopf; $19). Two characters—one black, one white—confront long-held beliefs.

CITY OF LIGHT by Cyrus Colter (Thunders Mouth Press; $12.95). A young African-American man comes to terms with the psychic wounds of his racially mixed background.

CLOTEL by William Wells-Brown (Citadel Press; $7.95). The story of a mulatto woman slave who ends her tragic life by drowning in the Potomac River as she is being pursued by a gang of whites.

CLOVER by Dori Saunders (Fawcett Columbine; $8). Clover, a ten-year-old girl is left in the care of her white step-mother when her father tragically dies just after the marriage ceremony. This story, set in small-town South Carolina, chronicles the sometimes bewildering relationship between woman and child.

COLLECTED STORIES OF CHARLES W. CHESTNUTT edited and with an introduction by William L. Andrews (Mentor Books; $5.99). Charles Chestnutt published his first short story in an 1887 issue of the *Atlantic Monthly*—an authentic innovative tale of hoodoo in the Old South told by a shrewd ex-slave. His later stories went on to expose the anguish of mixed-race men and women and the consequences of racial hatred, mob violence, and moral compromise. This important collection contains all the stories in Chestnutt's two published volumes.

THE COLOR PURPLE by Alice Walker (Washington Square Press; $5.95). Winner of the Pulitzer Prize and the American Book Award for Fiction. Life wasn't easy for Celie, but she knew how to survive, needing little to get by. Then her husband's lover, a flamboyant blues singer, barrels into her world and gives Celie the courage to ask for more.

COLORSTRUCK by Benita Porter (B.Q. Press; $24.95). A chronicle of the lives of black fraternal twins who look white and suffer the anguish that America's preoccupation with color causes them.

THE COTILLION by John Oliver Killens (Ballantine; $3.50). Yoruba Evelyn Lovejoy is a girl caught between two worlds: the world of 1960s Harlem where everything is black, hip, and funky and the uptight, plastic world that her mother has created. The Grand Cotillion offers Yoruba the chance to enter bourgeois black society—a place that is usually off limits to girls from Harlem.

DAUGHTERS by Paulie Marshall (Atheneum; $19.95). Set in New York City and the West Indies, *Daughters* presents us with a complex and vivid family, the MacKenzies and the host of friends, attendants, and lovers who surround them. At the center is Ursa MacKenzie, a young and professional black woman making a life and career for herself in New York. The book is not only about Ursa's life in the fast lane and proving ground of Manhattan, it is also the story of Ursa's struggle to come to terms with her family back in the West Indies, especially her father.

DEVIL IN A BLUE DRESS by Walter Mosley (W.W. Norton; $18.95). The time is 1948; the town is Los Angeles; the hero is Easy Rawlins, a tough black war veteran just out of a job at a defense plant. The mortgage payment is coming due, so Easy takes on some detective work. The assignment: find the whereabouts of blonde femme fatale, Daphne Monet.

DISAPPEARING ACTS by Terry McMillan (Pocket Books $8.95). Zora is a college-educated schoolteacher. Franklin barely finished high school and is a chronically unemployed construction worker. Their romance has delicious highs and heartbreaking lows. A sometimes joyous, sometimes tragic story of an African-American man and woman in love.

DIVINE DAYS by Leon Forrest (Another Chicago Press; $32.50). A saga that charts the homecoming revelations of a recent army dischargee and would-be playwright during a consciousness raising odyssey.

THE DOWRY by Ginger Whitaker (Holloway House; $3.50). Carrie Brown was young, beautiful, and a mystery to the townspeople. Left motherless at birth, she was sheltered her entire life by an overprotective and bitter father, the deacon of the Deliverance Church. People watched her from a distance, knowing about her, but never really knowing her. For Jimmy McCormack, Carrie was a goal, a desire he would pay anything to obtain.

EROTIQUE NOIRE/BLACK EROTICA edited by Miriam DeCosta-Willis, Reginald Martin, and Roseann P. Bell (Doubleday/Anchor Books; $27.50). An anthology of black erotica featuring stories and poems by prominent black writers.

FALLING LEAVES OF IVY by Yolanda Joe (Longmeadow Press; $18.95). A tale of murder, mystery, and suspense involving an interracial group of college friends.

FRAGMENTS THAT REMAIN by Steve Corbin (Alyson; $19.95). A black actor deals with his dysfunctional family while confronting racism from his white lover and the gay community.

FREE by Marsha Hunt (Dutton; $20). The year is 1913. The place is Germantown, a small Quaker and German immigrant community in Pennsylvania. The Emancipation Proclamation is fifty years old, but relationships between whites and blacks are tense, dramatic, and complex.

GOING TO MEET THE MAN by James Baldwin (Dell; $4.95). This brilliant collection of short stories contains truth telling and explosive narration. From largely autobiographical tales that create a vivid portrait of Harlem to stunning, sensual, violent tales of psychological and racial strife, this is a work of raw power and electrifying energy.

THE HARD TO CATCH MERCY by William Baldwin (Algonquin; $19.95). This comic novel debunks myths of family history, race relations, and religion in the post-Civil War South.

HARLEM by Tim McCanlies (Holloway House; $2.50). It was the end of Prohibition and Lenox Avenue was the place where sophisticates went to play. It was also the place where white gangsters and crooked cops came to collect their pound of flesh. When bandleader Sam Webster and his band open their own nightclub, they soon find themselves caught in the middle with guns coming at them from every direction. McCanlies has beautifully captured the Harlem of the 1930s, that era just before black performers "moved downtown."

HER OWN PLACE by Dori Sanders (Algonquin; $16.95). The only child of South Carolina tenant farmers and still in her teens when she marries, Mae Lee Barnes saves her wages from a job at a munitions plant, buys farmland of her own, and waits for her husband's return from World War II. He leaves, returns, and leaves again. Eventually he is gone for good, but not until Mae Lee is left with five children to raise and a farm to run by herself.

IF BEALE STREET COULD TALK by James Baldwin (Dell; $5.99). Fonny, a talented young artist, finds himself unjustly arrested and locked in New York's infamous Tombs. But his girl friend, Tish, is determined to free him and to have his baby in this starkly realistic tale.

INVISIBLE MAN by Ralph Ellison (Vintage Books; $10). A classic work that reveals the human universals hidden within the plight of those who are black and American.

IVY by Clyde Bolton (Holloway House; $3.95). Ivy is the tale of a grit poor, adolescent black girl orphaned in Georgia just before the beginning of the civil rights movement. Her personal struggle is set against the backdrop of the struggle to subdue American apartheid.

JAZZ by Toni Morrison (Knopf; $21.00). A story of romance, determination, and a community, set in Harlem more than fifty years ago.

JOY by Marsha Hunt (Dutton; $19.95). A richly moving, often shocking story told in the words of Baby Palatine, surrogate mother of Joy Bang, a black singer whose death sets this tale in motion. Why did the lovely, talented Joy die at too early an age? How did she die? And what is the real meaning of her death? These questions must be answered, and Baby Palatine's journey to the funeral becomes a soul-wrenching search for the truth.

LET THE DEAD BURY THEIR DEAD by Randall Kenan (Harcourt, Brace, Jovanovich; $19.95). A collection of twelve short stories set in and around the fictional town of Tims Creek and rooted in oral history, scripture, and fantasy.

LUCY by Jamaica Kincaid (Plume; $8.95). Lucy is nineteen, a vinegary, quick-tongued au pair from the West Indies who has left behind her island girlhood for a fierce awakening in urban North America.

MAMA by Terry McMillan (Washington Square Press; $9). Tale of a spunky, sexy, resourceful woman raising her children alone after getting rid of her womanizing husband.

MASTERPIECES OF AFRICAN-AMERICAN LITERATURE edited by Frank Magill (HarperCollins; $40). Synopses of 142 classic works spanning more than a century by a wide range of African-American authors.

MERIDIAN by Alice Walker (Pocket Books; $4.95). Set in the 1960s as the old rules of southern society collapse, this is the story of one woman's lonely battle to reaffirm her own humanity—and that of all her people.

MIDDLE PASSAGE by Charles Johnson (Atheneum; $17.95). Winner of the 1990 National Book Award. The year is 1830 and Rutherford Calhoun, a newly freed slave, finds himself forced into marriage with a Boston schoolteacher. To escape from wedlock and his considerable debts, Rutherford stows away on the first available ship. To his shock and horror, he learns that the vessel is a slave ship bound for Africa.

A MISSISSIPPI FAMILY by Barbara Johnson with Mary Sikora (Holloway House; $2.50). The journey from poverty to relative comfort of a Mississippi family. As in *Roots*, the story is based on the remembrances passed on generation to generation by the members of a family.

NOT WITHOUT LAUGHTER by Langston Hughes (Collier/Macmillan; $6.95). In 1926 Langston Hughes said "we younger Negro artists who create now intend to express ourselves without fear or shame. If white people are pleased we are glad. If they are not, it doesn't matter." His statement was hailed as a manifesto by the artists and intellectuals of the Harlem Renaissance, and its writer became a symbol of the newly awakened black consciousness. In 1930 the gifted young poet released this book, his long awaited first novel. This poignant story of a boy growing to manhood in a small Kansas town has become a pioneering classic of black literature.

NOUVELLE SOUL by Barbara Summers (Amistad Press; $22.95). A collection of short stories on contemporary African-American life.

ONE DAY WHEN I WAS LOST by James Baldwin (Dell; $4.95). A film scenario based on the *Autobiography of Malcom X*.

A RED DEATH: AN EASY RAWLINS MYSTERY by Walter Mosley (Pocket Books; $4.99). It is 1953 in Red-baiting, blacklisting Los Angeles. Easy Rawlins is out of "the hurting business" and into the housing business when a racist IRS agent nails him for tax evasion. In a deal to get out from under the charge, Rawlins agrees to infiltrate the First African Baptist Church and spy on alleged communist union organizer Chaim Wenzler. That's when the murders begin.

REUNION by Mark Allen Boone (Holloway House; $2.95). The story of two friends and one man's determination to find his origin. It is a story of the kind of deep, abiding friendship that is stronger than blood. Levi Merriweather and Wesley Luckett had such a friendship. They shared everything, even the same woman. But like the tides, which ebb and flow, friends can drift apart.

SONG OF SOLOMON by Toni Morrison (Plume; $7.95). An unusual dramatic story of the black experience replete with unrequited loves, bitter hates, intense loyalties, and fantastic events.

SULA by Toni Morrison (Plume; $5.95). This rich and moving novel traces the lives of two black heroines—from their growing up together in a small Ohio town, through their sharply divergent paths of womanhood, to their ultimate confrontation and reconciliation.

TAR BABY by Toni Morrison (Plume; $10.00). The story of a young, black career woman who learns lessons about life during a short stay on an island in the Caribbean.

TEMPLE OF MY FAMILIAR by Alice Walker (Harcourt Brace Jovanovich; $19.95). A controversial novel which protests the barbaric practice of female circumsion in an African community.

THEIR EYES WERE WATCHING GOD by Zora Neale Hurston (University of Illinois Press; $5.95). A young woman named Janie gets into an arranged marriage to an old farmer who can't see any further than his plow and does not realize her deep unhappiness. When the farmer realizes that Janie doesn't return his love, he tries to destroy her spirit.

VANISHING ROOMS by Melvin Dixon (Dutton; $18.95). A powerful novel exploring the issues of homophobia and racism. Jesse Durand is a black dancer whose life is suddenly shattered when his white boyfriend, Metro, becomes the victim of a murderous assault. Ruella is the woman to whom he turns in his grief. Although Ruella feels his pain, she chooses to ignore his homosexuality in hopes that he will ease her own emotional and sexual isolation. A challenging look at the high cost of passion.

WAITING TO EXHALE by Terry McMillan (Viking; $22.00). Savannah Jackson, Bernadine Harris, Robin Stokes, and Gloria Matthews are four successful African-American women who lean on each other while coming to terms with middle age and their continuing search for an ideal man who will take their breath away. Through their complex friendships, McMillan gives us a poignant and fiercely accurate portrait of modern female camaraderie.

THE WAYS OF WHITE FOLKS by Langston Hughes (Vintage; $8.95). Perhaps more than any other writer, Langston Hughes made the white America of the 1920s and thirties aware of the black culture thriving in its midst. These Hughes stories are messages from black America. They contain sharply etched vignettes of its daily life, cruelly accurate portrayals of black people colliding—ometimes humorously, more often tragically—with whites.

WHITE BUTTERFLY: AN EASY RAWLINS MYSTERY by Walter Mosley (W.W. Norton; $19.95). The year is 1956 and no one in official Los Angeles is much bothered as a serial killer proceeds to murder three black bar girls, leaving a distinctive mark each time. Then a white stripper, Cyndi Starr, known on stage as "The White Butterfly," is murdered in the same manner. It turns out that Starr was not just any stripper, she was a UCLA coed and the daughter of a politically powerful prosecutor. Suddenly, the heat is on to find the killer.

YORUBA GIRL DANCING by Simi Bedford (Viking Penguin; $19). The story of a girl's exile from her Nigerian homeland and her coming of age in an English boarding school.

YOU CAN'T KEEP A GOOD WOMAN DOWN by Alice Walker (Harvest/HBJ; $5.95). Fourteen provocative and often humorous stories that show women oppressed but not defeated. These are modern stories about love, lust, fame, and cultural thievery; the perils of pornography, abortion, and rape; the delight of new lovers; and the rediscovery of old friends.

YOUR BLUES AIN'T LIKE MINE by Bebe Moore Campbell (Putnam; $24.95). This novel set in Mississippi reflects on the tragic slaying of a fourteen year old youth from Chicago (a figure reminiscent of Emmett Till) and on the complex chain of events touched off by his murder. A story of murder, love, and passion in the Mississippi Delta.

Fiction Index (BY AUTHOR)

Austin, Doris Jean	*After The Garden*
Baldwin, James	*Going To Meet The Man*
	If Beale Street Could Talk
	One Day When I Was Lost
Baldwin, William	*The Hard To Catch Mercy*
Bedford, Simi	*Yoruba Girl Dancing*
Bolton, Clyde	*Ivy*
Boone, Mark Allen	*Reunion*
Campbell, Bebe Moore	*Your Blues Ain't Like Mine*
Chapman, Abraham	*Black Voices*
Chestnutt, Charles W.	*Collected Stories of Charles W. Chestnutt*
Colter, Cyrus	*City of Light*
Corbin, Steve	*Fragments That Remain*

De-Costa, Willis — *Erotique Noire/Black Erotica*

Dixon, Melvin — *Vanishing Rooms*

Ellison, Ralph — *Invisible Man*

Forrest, Leon — *Divine Days*

Golden, Marita — *And Do Remember Me*

Hughes, Langston — *Not Without Laughter*
The Ways of White Folks

Hunt, Marsha — *Free*
Joy

Hurston, Zora Neale — *Their Eyes Were Watching God*

Joe, Yolanda — *Falling Leaves of Ivy*

Johnson, Barbara — *A Mississippi Family*

Johnson, Charles — *Middle Passage*

Kenan, Randall — *Let The Dead Bury Their Dead*

Killens, John Oliver — *The Cotillion*

Kincaid, Jamaica — *Lucy*

Magill, Frank — *Masterpieces of African-American*
Literature

Marshall, Paule — *Brown Girl, Brownstones*
Daughters

McCanlies, Tim — *Harlem*

McMillan, Terry — *Breaking Ice*
Disappearing Acts
Mama
Waiting To Exhale

Morrison, Toni	*Beloved*
	Jazz
	Song of Solomon
	Sula
	Tar Baby
Mosley, Walter	*Devil In a Blue Dress:*
	An Easy Rawlins Mystery
	A Red Death: An Easy Rawlins Mystery
	White Butterfly: An Easy Rawlins
	Mystery
Phillips, Caryl	*Cambridge*
Porter, Benita	*Colorstruck*
Saunders, Dori	*Clover*
	Her Own Place
Summers, Barbara	*Nouvelle Soul*
Walker, Alice	*The Color Purple*
	Meridian
	Temple of my Familiar
	You Can't Keep A Good Woman Down
Wells-Brown, William	*Clotel*
Whitaker, Ginger	*The Dowry*

Health and Fitness

THE BLACK HEALTH LIBRARY GUIDE TO STROKE AND HEART DISEASE by Lafayette Singleton, M.D. with Kirk Johnson and Linda Villarosa (Henry Holt; $8.95). A discussion of why black people are at particular risk and preventive measures that can be taken.

History

THE AFRICAN-AMERICANS edited by Charles Collins and David Cohen (Viking; $45). An illustrated volume recounting the stories of heroes and achievers in American life.

AFRO-AMERICAN HISTORY: THE MODERN ERA by Herbert Aptheker (Citadel Press; $7.95). Covers important events and data from the Washington-Du Bois Conference of 1904 to the Watts ghetto uprising in August 1965.

BLACK BRITTANIA: A HISTORY OF BLACKS IN BRITAIN by Edward Scobie (Johnson Publishing Co.; $7.95). The story of the blacks in Britain from the seventeenth to the twentieth centuries. The author, a West Indian journalist who worked in London, adds his own experience to more than ten years of historical research. The book sheds light on a story long in the shadows of history.

BLACK CALIFORNIA: THE HISTORY OF AFRICAN-AMERICANS IN THE GOLDEN STATE by B. Gordon Wheeler (Hippocrene Books; $22.50). The story of black people in California is a combination of the tragic and the heroic, of denial and affirmation. Most of all, it is the record of a tidal force in the building of America's thirty-first state.

BLACK SELF-DETERMINATION: A CULTURAL HISTORY OF AFRICAN-AMERICAN RESISTANCE by V.P. Franklin with a foreword by U.S. Commission on Civil Rights member Mary Frances Berry (Lawrence Hill Books; $14.95). This is an in-depth analysis of black mass movements from the late eighteenth century to the twentieth century.

DOCUMENTARY HISTORY OF THE NEGRO PEOPLE IN THE U.S. by Herbert Aptheker (Citadel Press; Six Volumes at $16.95 each). Black Americans tell the story of the nation's major historical events through their own experiences. These volumes start in colonial times and end as Martin Luther King emerges as the clarion voice of the civil rights movement. They are the result of a decade of research in archives, libraries, and repositories, as well as Aptheker's sifting through hundreds of newspapers, leaflets, broadsides, manuscript letters, and books.

FREDERICK DOUGLASS by William S. McFeely (Touchstone; $14). An incisive portrait of the charismatic social crusader. A self-taught, escaped slave, Douglass emerged as the abolition movement's most stirring orator and went on to become an author, newspaper publisher, bank president, and diplomat.

WADE IN THE WATER: GREAT MOMENTS IN BLACK AMERICAN HISTORY by Lerone Bennett Jr. (Johnson Publishing Co.; $17.95) Fifteen dramatic episodes in black history proved to be turning points in the shaping of two Americas, one black and one white. In this volume the reader will feel the complete meaning of the black tradition as summed up in the spiritual "Wade in the Water."

WHY WE CAN'T WAIT by Martin Luther King, Jr. (Mentor; $2.95) In this important book Dr. King told America why the black man could not longer wait for civil rights. He traces the history of the African-American's fight for equality back to its beginning some three centuries ago and then goes on to explain why things had to come to a head on the streets of Birmingham.

WORLD'S GREAT MEN OF COLOR by J.A. Rogers (Collier Books; $13.95). Did you know that Aesop was black? This trailblazing study explodes the myth that blacks played only minor roles in world history. The author has devoted more than half a century to researching the lives of hundreds of individuals and has reclaimed several important individuals for black history.

How-To

KWANZAA: EVERYTHING YOU ALWAYS WANTED TO KNOW BUT DIDN'T KNOW WHERE TO ASK by Cedric McClester (Gumbs & Thomas $5.95). A complete explanation of Kwanzaa and how to celebrate it.

Humor

BILL COSBY: CHILDHOOD by Bill Cosby (G. P. Putnam's; $14.95). Childhood is Bill Cosby country. In this entertaining and endearing book, Cosby holds forth with the most marvelous stories he has ever told about his childhood. And, in a delightful counterpoint to his own now legendary childhood, Cosby offers his hilarious but incisive observations about kids today.

TIME FLIES by Bill Cosby (Doubleday; $15.95). The comedian brings his unique warmth, wisdom, and wit to the subject of aging. Here are the trials and tribulations of mid-life; the aches and pains and the battle of the bulge. It happens to the best of us, and Cosby delivers his hilarious observations in his own style.

Justice and Law

BLACK ROBES, WHITE JUSTICE: WHY OUR LEGAL SYSTEM DOESN'T WORK FOR BLACKS by Judge Bruce Wright (Lyle Stuart; $12.95). The author, a New York State Supreme Court Justice and a black man, argues that our legal system is fundamentally unfair towards African-Americans. He documents this assertion with many cases drawn from his long experience as a lawyer and judge. The subjects covered include affirmative action, police power, law schools, the U.S. Constitution, and the deeply ingrained prejudices of many white judges. In the aftermath of the Rodney King trials and the L.A. riots, much of what Judge Wright has written is more timely and relevant than ever.

EMANCIPATION: THE MAKING OF A BLACK LAWYER, 1844-1944 by J. Clay Smith, Jr., foreword by Justice Thurgood Marshall (University of Pennsylvania Press; $56.95). A hundred year history of the achievements of African-American lawyers, revealing the roles they played in the judicial, political, and social emancipation of their fellow black citizen.

RACE-ING JUSTICE, EN-GENDERING POWER: ESSAYS ON ANITA HILL, CLARENCE THOMAS AND THE CONSTRUCTION OF SOCIAL REALITY edited by Toni Morrison (Pantheon; $15). A collection of eighteen essays by prominent scholars—black, white, male and female—examining the social, sexual, racial, political, professional and personal ramifications that were the result of sexual harassment charges by University of Oklahoma law professor Anita Hill during the confirmation hearings of Supreme Court Justice Clarence Thomas.

THE RODNEY KING REBELLION by Dr. Brenda Wall (African-American Images; $9.95). Dr. Wall, a clinical psychologist, presents a factual review of the King arrest, trial, and the aftermath. This analysis compares the uprising by the underprivileged of South Central L.A. to the uprising by African-American college students at two major universities.

WHY L.A. HAPPENED: IMPLICATIONS OF THE '92 LOS ANGELES REBELLION edited by Hadi Madhubuti (Third World Press; $14.95). A collection of essays by a cross section of scholars and commentators that examines the riots following the acquittal of four white police officers in the beating of black motorist Rodney King.

Military

BROTHERS: BLACK SOLDIERS IN THE NAM by Stanley Goff and Robert Sanders with Clark Smith (Berkeley; $3.99). The authors both served in Vietnam and in this work try to portray the unique experience of blacks fighting in America's most controversial war.

TAPS FOR A JIM CROW ARMY: LETTERS FROM BLACK SOLDIERS IN WORLD WAR II edited by Philip McGuire (University Press of Kentucky; $19). The book chronicles the reactions of black American soldiers to the discrimination they endured in the U.S. Army.

UNDYING GLORY: THE STORY OF THE MASSACHU- SETTS 54TH REGIMENT by Clinton Cox (City Sun;

$14.95). New York reporter Clinton Cox, twice nominated for the Pulitzer Prize, relates the story of African-American soldiers of the Civil War who fought to release their brothers and sisters from slavery. The "Glory" regiment is brought to life by archival black and white photos.

Music

AMATEUR NIGHT AT THE APOLLO by Ralph Cooper with Steve Dougherty (HarperCollins; $25). The book paints a vivid picture of fifty years of American music set against a Harlem backdrop. Swing, bebop, R&B and rock and roll every important trend in popular music began in the black community and was played on stage at the Apollo.

BLACK MUSIC by Imamu Baraka (Morrow; $8.95). Essays, profiles, and liner notes written by Baraka on the modern jazz scene in the 1960s and seventies.

BLUES PEOPLE: NEGRO MUSIC IN WHITE AMERICA by Imamu Baraka (William Morrow; $9.95). This book traces music from the songs of slavery to Coltrane.

THE DEATH OF RHYTHM AND BLUES by Nelson George (Plume; $8.95). A passionate, provocative book which tells the complete story of black music in the last fifty years.

REPEAL OF THE BLUES: HOW BLACK ENTERTAINERS INFLUENCED CIVIL RIGHTS by Alan Pomerance (Citadel Press; $17.95). Traces the roles of blacks in the performing arts starting in 1932. It follows the course of show business history from that point to the present and analyzes the performers' role in the quest for civil rights.

SWING OUT: GREAT NEGRO DANCE BANDS by Gene Fernett (Da Capo Press; $14.95). The richness of jazz history cannot be fully appreciated without reading about the black dance bands that dominated jazz throughout the first half of this century. These are inside stories about such notables as Louis Armstrong, Ella Fitzgerald, Fats Waller, Lionel Hampton, Cab Calloway, and Earl Hines with more than 150 magnificent photographs.

Philosophy

PHILOSOPHY AND OPINION OF MARCUS GARVEY (Antheneum; $16). A collection of the thoughts and words of the great early 20th century leader, edited by his second wife, Amy Jacques-Garvey with an introduction by Robert A. Hill.

THE SOULS OF BLACK FOLK by W.E.B. Du Bois (Signet Classic; $2.95). An afrocentric thinker, writer, and scholar in a time of absolute white dominance, Du Bois urged the establishment of an "all-black party" and preached the need for black conscious self realization.

Photography

DIZZY: JOHN BURKS GILLESPIE IN HIS 75TH YEAR compiled and edited by Lee Tanner (Pomegranate Artbooks; $25). A homage to Dizzy Gillespie and his career which began in the 1940s.

GENERATIONS IN BLACK AND WHITE by Carl Van Vechten (University of Georgia Press; $29.95). This portfolio of eighty-three portraits constitutes a stunning celebration of three decades of African-American achievement.

MALCOLM X: THE GREAT PHOTOGRAPHS by Thulani Davis (Stewart, Tabori & Chang; $24.95). One hundred and ten handsome duotone photographs by Gordon Parks, Eve Arnold, and Henri Cartier-Bresson.

MALCOLM X: MAKE IT PLAIN by John A. Williams and the Malcolm X: Make It Plain Production Team (Viking; $35). This is a companion volume to a documentary film. Includes a major collection of photographs of the great leader.

Poetry

THE BLACK POETS edited by Dudley Randall (Bantam Books; $5.95). This book offers a full range of black poetry and presents many poets in depth. In some cases it presents aspects of a poet's work that have been overlooked. For example, Gwendolyn Brooks is represented not only by poems on racial and domestic themes, but is revealed as a writer of superb love lyrics. Turning away from white models and returning to their roots has freed black poets to create a new poetry. This book records their progress.

Politics

BLACK POWER: THE POLITICS OF LIBERATION by Toure and Charles V. Hamilton (Vintage Books; $10). Exposes systematic racism in America and presents a framework for racial reform. The authors call for African-Americans to unite, recognize their heritage, and build a sense of community so that they can bargain from a position of strength in a pluralistic society.

BY ANY MEANS NECESSARY (Pathfinders; $15.95).
This is a collection of Malcolm X's speeches, interviews, and
letters from the last years of his life and sheds new light on
the evolution of his views on political alliances, women's
rights, capitalism, and socialism.

DESTRUCTION OF BLACK CIVILIZATION by
Chancellor Williams (Third World Press; $16.95).
The author discusses his theory of the planned destruction
of the African world.

**DOMESTIC ALLEGORIES OF POLITICAL DESIRE:
THE BLACK HEROINE'S TEXT AT THE TURN OF THE
CENTURY** by Claudia Tate (Oxford University Press; $35).
A critical analysis of the black women writers of the late nine-
teenth century whose fictional writings reveal the political
aspirations of black Americans.

**JUST PERMANENT INTERESTS: BLACK AMERICANS
IN CONGRESS 1870-1991** by William L. Clay (Amistad
Press; $24.95). As the senior member of the Missouri
Congressional delegation and a founding member of the
Congressional Black Caucus, William L. Clay shares thirty-
four years of experiences and insight into the political process
and the roles that black elected officials have played from the
post Civil War era to the present.

MALCOLM A TO X: THE MAN AND HIS IDEAS by David
Gallen (Carroll & Graf; $8.95). Introduces the reader to the
basic views of Malcolm X in a readily accessible, alphabetical
format that covers a wide range of topics. Here are memo-
rable comments, often in Malcolm X's own words on such

items as ballots or bullets, the Ku Klux Klan, news media and segregation.

MARTIN & MALCOLM & AMERICA by James H. Cone (Orbis Books; $22.95). Popular images of Martin Luther King and Malcolm X seldom acknowledge their movement toward each other and their break with earlier deeply held convictions. This book is about the philosophies of King and Malcolm X—their relationship to each other and their meanings for America.

THE SOULS OF BLACK FOLK by W. E. B. Du Bois (Signet; $4.95). Primarily a historical document which delves into the "Negro Problem" as it existed immediately following the Civil War. Although much of the book is dated, it still stands as a monument to the black man's struggle in this country.

A TESTAMENT OF HOPE: THE ESSENTIAL WRITINGS AND SPEECHES OF MARTIN LUTHER KING JR. edited by James M. Washington (HarperSanFrancisco; $16.95). Here, in the only major one-volume collection of his writings, speeches, interviews, and autobiographical reflections is King on nonviolence, social policy, integration, black nationalism, and the ethics of love and hope.

Psychology

IN THE COMPANY OF MY SISTERS by Julia A. Boyd (Dutton; $18.00). The first book by a black psychotherapist ever to address the emotional issues and realities of black women's lives, this book brings a message of rebirth and renewal to every black woman who seeks her most intimate self.

THE SILENT TWINS by Marjorie Wallace (Ballantine; $3.95). This is the astonishing true tale of June and Jennifer Gibbons, identical twins whose silent, antisocial exterior hid a rich, vast, creative life. From their early childhood through their twenties, they spoke only to each other in a secret language, building an elaborate fantasy life. From their self-imposed isolation, they were catapulted into the hormonal havoc of adolescence—plunging into a wild spree that ultimately led to their incarceration in a hospital for the criminally insane.

Race

BLACK LIKE ME by John Howard Griffin (Signet; $4.99). The story of a white man who underwent a series of medical treatments to change his skin color temporarily to black. The experiences he encountered are a scathing indictment of a racist society.

THE COLOR COMPLEX: THE POLITICS OF SKIN COLOR AMONG AFRICAN-AMERICANS by Kathy Russell, Midge Wilson and Ronald Hall (Harcourt Brace Jovanovich; $21.95). An examination of how skin color plays a role in the socioeconomic status, relationships, and professional lives of black Americans.

FACES AT THE BOTTOM OF THE WELL: THE PERMANENCE OF RACISM by Derrick Bell (Basic Books, $20). The controversial Harvard Law School professor uses allegory and historical example to present a radical vision of the persistence of racism today.

PRISONERS OF OUR PAST: A CRITICAL LOOK AT SELF-DEFEATING ATTITUDES WITHIN THE BLACK COMMUNITY by James Davison, Jr., Ph.D. (Birch Lane Press; $17.95) A black conservative argues that African-Americans have contributed significantly to the inequities we face.

RACE MATTERS by Cornel West (Beacon Press; $15). A collection of essays on racial issues addressing affirmative action, the legacy of Malcolm X, black-jewish relations and black sexuality.

Reference

THE BLACK 100: A RANKING OF THE MOST INFLUENTIAL AFRICAN-AMERICANS, PAST AND PRESENT by Columbus Salley (Citadel Press; $21.95). After extensive thought and research, author and educator Dr. Columbus Salley has selected the one hundred most influential African-Americans of all time and then ranked them according to their contributions to the struggle for equality.

ENCYCLOPEDIA OF BLACK AMERICA Edited by W. Augustus Low and Virgil A. Clift (Da Capo Press; $35.00). This first encyclopedic volume on black America fills a long neglected need. More than eighty contributors, all experts in their field, have cooperated to make this a readable and reliable reference source representing the totality of the past and present of African-Americans. The easy access A-to-Z format allows the reader to locate individuals, topics, organizations such as the NAACP, SNCC, Black Panther Party, and others.

LIFT EVERY VOICE AND SING by James Weldon Johnson and Elizabeth Catlett (Walker; $14.95). Combines Catlett's linocuts with the lyrics of the song that has been adopted as the African-American national anthem; proceeds will be donated to Hale House.

1999 FACTS ABOUT BLACKS: A SOURCEBOOK OF AFRICAN-AMERICAN ACCOMPLISHMENT by Raymond M. Corbin (Beecham House; $10.95). The contributions of African-American men and women are proudly documented in this compact yet comprehensive reference work. Each entry reveals another fact about black achievement that conventional histories have consistently overlooked.

Religion

THE BLACK CHURCH IN THE AMERICAN EXPERIENCE by C. Eric Lincoln and Lawrence H. Mamiya (Duke University Press; $47.50 hardcover; $18.95 paperback). An exhaustive study of the religious and social role of the seven major black denominations—African Methodist Episcopal; African Methodist Episcopal Zion; Christian Methodist Episcopal; National Baptist Convention USA, Inc; National Baptist Convention of America Unincorporated; the Progressive National Baptist Convention; and the Church of God in Christ.

Self Help and Recovery

IN THE SPIRIT: THE INSPIRATIONAL WRITINGS OF SUSAN L. TAYLOR (Amistad Press; $14.95). A collection of essays written for black women over the last decade by the editor of *Essence* magazine.

NURTURING YOUNG BLACK MALES by Ronald B. Mincy (Urban Institute Press; $19.95). Describes programs that have kept black teenagers from crime, drugs, and unemployment.

WHAT BLACK PEOPLE SHOULD DO NOW: DISPATCHES FROM NEAR THE VANGUARD by Ralph Wiley (Ballantine; $22). A collection of essays on race, culture, politics, and black survival.

Theater, Film and Television

BLACK HOLLYWOOD: FROM 1970 TO TODAY by Gary Null (Citadel Press; $17.95). Featuring nearly seven hundred photographs, this is a book about the radical changes seen in Hollywood over the past twenty years. In that time, African-American performers like Bill Cosby, Eddie Murphy, Denzel Washington, and Danny Glover have become major stars.

BLACK MUSICAL THEATRE: FROM COONTOWN TO DREAMGIRLS by Allen Woll (Da Capo Press; $13.95). While theatergoers are generally familiar with the names of such pioneers as George M. Cohan, Irving Berlin, and

Jerome Kern, the names of their black counterparts—Will Marion Cook, George Walker, and Bob Cole, among others—are virtually unknown today. Allen Woll remedies that neglect in this book, providing a thoroughly researched account of the evolution of black musical theater from the turn of the century to the present day.

BROWN SUGAR: EIGHTY YEARS OF AMERICA'S BLACK FEMALE SUPERSTARS by Donald Bogle (Da Capo Press; $15.95). From the turn of the twentieth century to its last few decades, a striking lineup of breathtaking black women have dazzled us with their energy, talent, and style. Lavishly illustrated, this book is filled with the stories of America's black female superstars—Ma Rainey, Ethel Waters, Josephine Baker, Lena Horne, the Supremes, Donna Summer, Katherine Dunham, Hazel Scott, Marian Anderson, Dinah Washington, Pearl Bailey, Dorothy Dandridge, Leontyne Price, Aretha Franklin, Nina Simone, Tina Turner. A stirring narration of the triumphant struggle of these women to make it in the entertainment industry against overwhelming odds.

True Crime

DELIBERATE INDIFFERENCE: A STORY OF MURDER AND RACIAL INJUSTICE by Howard Swindle (Viking; $22.50). On Christmas Day 1987, a black man named Loyal Garner, Jr., drove down the wrong road in East Texas and was pulled over by a white police chief. He was taken to jail, beaten unconscious, and hospitalized—afterwards, officers came up with a cover story. Although witnesses swore that he was murdered, the policemen were summarily acquitted by a hometown jury. Only after prosecutors in another county wrested control of the case was justice served. This book is a profoundly disturbing investigation of sanctioned murder and a miscarriage of justice.

THE JUDAS FACTOR: THE PLOT TO KILL MALCOLM x by Karl Evanzz (Thunder's Mouth Press; $22.95). An analysis of the role the intelligence community played in the assassination of Malcolm X.

MALCOLM X: THE ASSASSINATION by Michael Friedly (Carroll & Graf; $10.95). By February 21, 1965, Malcolm X knew the end was near and it showed. Nearly a year had passed since he had severed his ties with the black separatist Nation of Islam and its self-proclaimed "Messenger of Allah" known as Elijah Muhammad, and for months Malcolm had been outrunning armed Muslims who wanted to kill him for breaking with the messenger and defaming his name. Although the author, Michael Friedly is definitely not Malcolm-friendly, this book is important because it closely examines the stories of Norman 3X Butler and Thomas 15X Johnson, the two Muslim brothers who were wrongly convicted of the crime.

PORTRAIT OF A RACIST: THE MAN WHO KILLED MEDGAR EVERS by Reed Massengill (St. Martin's; $22.95). Profiles Byron de la Beckwith, the man who committed the heinous crime and walked away scot-free.

Women's Studies

BLACK WOMEN FOR BEGINNERS by Saundra Sharp, illustrated by Beverly Hawkins Hall (Writers and Readers; $9.95). An introduction in comic-book style to the issues and identities of women of African descent.

BLACK WOMEN IN WHITE AMERICA: A DOCUMENTARY HISTORY edited by Gerda Lerner (Vintage; $12). Black women tell not only what it is like to be oppressed but also how they have managed to survive.

DAUGHTERS OF AFRICA (Pantheon; $35). An anthology of oral and written literature by women of African descent from ancient Egyptian Queen Hatshepsut to contemporary writers such as Terry McMillan and Alice Walker, edited with an introduction by Margaret Busby.

THE HOTTEST WATER IN CHICAGO by Gayle Pemberton (Faber & Faber; $19.95). Sixteen autobiographical essays on family, race, time, and American culture by the director of the Afro-American studies program at Princeton University.

READING BLACK, READING FEMINIST edited by Louis Gates Junior (Meridian; $14.95). An anthology of twenty-six essays and interviews touching on the works of key African-American women writers from Zora Neale Hurston to Jamaica Kincaid. Edited by one of the nation's foremost African-American scholars.

THEORIZING BLACK FEMINISM: THE VISIONARY PRAGMATISM OF BLACK WOMEN edited by Stanlie M. James and Abena P.A. Busia (Routledge; $49.95). A collection of essays by Patricia Williams, Johnnetta Cole, and others.

CHAPTER

2

Colleges and Universities

Higher education for African-Americans began right after the Civil War. The first colleges had to start with the basic reading and writing skills needed by men and women newly freed from bondage. Secondary level programs and college level courses were gradually added. Many schools also offered religion and vocational training. Graduate degree programs were added between 1930 and 1950. These historically black colleges still exist although they have moved from their makeshift sites (church basements, barns, etc.) that held the anxious ex-slaves to modern school complexes of various types and sizes. Unfortunately, since the 1960s, the black colleges have been struggling to survive.

The civil rights movement opened many doors for African-Americans. One of those doors led into the white college classroom. As a result, many middle class black parents began sending their children to prestigious white colleges and state universities, which left many of the historically black colleges in a serious financial bind. "Save the Black Colleges" campaigns have been extremely helpful but have not solved the problem.

To solve the problem, more black high school students and adults returning to school must turn to the black colleges. These institutions provide a source of ethnic pride, an opportunity to develop leadership skills, programs designed to meet the unique needs of the black community, and highly trained faculties.

Profiles of the following historically black colleges and universities are not designed to replace the school catalog. Call or write for free brochures, which describe areas of study, financial aid, and student activities.

ALABAMA AGRICULTURAL AND MECHANICAL (A&M) UNIVERSITY in Normal, Alabama, was founded in 1875. Beginning in 1876 and for many years thereafter, the school was influenced by its executive head, William Hooper Councill (born of slave parents), a prominent educator, editor, and associate of Booker T. Washington. LOCATION: Suburban campus in small city, 95 miles north of Birmingham. DEGREES OFFERED: AA, AS, BA, BS, MS, MBA, MEd, Ph.D. ANNUAL EXPENSES: Tuition and fees $1,298; $988 additional for out-of-state students. Room and board $2,036. Books and supplies $500. Other expenses $756. FALL TERM APPLICATIONS: $10 fee. No closing date. Priority given to applications received by May. Applicants notified on a rolling basis, must reply within 4 weeks. CONTACT: James O. Heyward, Director of Admissions, Alabama Agricultural and Mechanical University, P.O. Box 908, Normal, AL 35762 (205) 851-5245.

ALABAMA STATE UNIVERSITY (Montgomery) was founded at Salem in 1874 as the State Normal School and University for Colored Students and Teachers. It was the first state-supported institution for the training of black teachers in the United States. By the mid-1970s about two-thirds of all African-American teachers in Alabama were graduates of this university. LOCATION: Urban campus in small city, 91 miles south of Birmingham. DEGREES OFFERED: AA, AS, BA, BS, MA, MS, MEd. ANNUAL EXPENSES: Tuition and fees $1,268; $1,160 additional for out-of-state students. Room and board $1,991. Books and supplies $570. Other expenses $1,200. FALL TERM APPLICATIONS: No fee. Closing date August 1. Priority given to applications received by July 1. Applicants notified on a rolling basis. Interview recommended. Audition required for music applicants. Portfolio recommended for art applicants. Essay recommended. Deferred and early admission available. CONTACT: Debbie Moore, Enrollment Management, Alabama State University, 9115 Jackson Street, Montgomery, AL 36101 (205) 293-4291.

ALBANY STATE COLLEGE at Albany, Georgia, was founded in 1903 as the Albany Biblical and Manual Training Institute. The coeducational school traces its origins to Dr. Joseph Winthrop Holley, an educator who came to Albany seeking aid in the establishment of a school for Afro-American youth. With the financial help of the Hazard family of Rhode Island, and several of the leading white citizens of

Albany, Holley founded and maintained the institute. He remained its president until 1943. LOCATION: Urban campus in small city, 176 miles south of Atlanta. DEGREES OFFERED: AA, BA, BS, MS, MBA. ANNUAL EXPENSES: Tuition and fees $1,599; $2,478 additional for out-of-state students. Room and board $2,355. Books and supplies $520. Other expenses $650. FALL TERM APPLICATIONS: No fee. Closing date September 1. Applicants notified on a rolling basis. Must reply within 1 week. Interview required for academically weak applicants. Deferred and early admission available. CONTACT: Mrs. Patricia Price, Assistant Director of Admissions, Albany State College, 504 College Drive, Albany, GA 31705-2769 (912) 430-4650.

ALCORN STATE UNIVERSITY at Lorman, Mississippi, was founded in 1871 as a land grant institution and named in honor of a Reconstruction governor of the state. LOCATION: Rural campus in small town, 40 miles from Natchez and Vicksburg. DEGREES OFFERED: BA, BS, MS. ANNUAL EXPENSES: Tuition and fees $1,750; $1,182 additional for out-of-state students. Room and board $1,925. Books and supplies $400. Other expenses $900. FALL TERM APPLICATIONS: No fee. No closing date. Priority given to applications received by July 21. Applicants notified on a rolling basis. Interview required for nursing applicants. Audition required for music applicants. Deferred and early admission available. CONTACT: Albert Z. Johnson, Director of Admissions, Alcorn State University, Box 300, Lorman, MS 39096 (601) 877-6147.

ALLEN UNIVERSITY at Columbia, South Carolina, was founded in 1870 as Payne Institute in Cokesbury, South

Carolina by the African Methodist Episcopal church. Allen University was the first institution of higher learning for African-Americans in South Carolina. During its early years, it had to serve its students at all educational levels. At one time, a student might enter Allen in the first grade and leave as a college graduate. The grammar school was discontinued in the mid-1920s, and the high school ended with the graduating class of 1929. LOCATION: Urban campus in small city. DEGREES OFFERED: AA, BA, BS. ANNUAL EXPENSES: Tuition and fees $3,720. Room and board $2,900. Books and supplies $300. FALL TERM APPLICATIONS: $10 fee. May be waived for applicants with need. No closing date. Applicants notified on a rolling basis. Interview recommended. CONTACT: Ms. Shirley Fennell, Director of Admissions and Financial Aid, Allen University, 1530 Harden Street, Columbia, SC 29204 (803) 254-4165.

ARKANSAS BAPTIST COLLEGE at Little Rock, Arkansas, was founded in 1884 by the Baptist church. A small four-year coeducational college, it grants the bachelor's degree and provides liberal arts and teacher education curricula. The enrollment increased from 170 in 1970 to about 500 in 1975. LOCATION: Urban campus in small city, in downtown area. DEGREES OFFERED: AA, BA, BS. ANNUAL EXPENSES: Tuition and fees $1,670. Room and board $2,200. Books and supplies $600. Other expenses $850. FALL TERM APPLICATIONS: $10 fee. Closing date September 30. Applicants notified on a rolling basis beginning on or about June 30. Interview recommended. Deferred admission available. CONTACT: Mrs. Annie A. Hightower, Registrar/Director of Admissions, Arkansas Baptist Church, 1600 Bishop Street, Little Rock, AR 72202 (501) 374-7856.

BARBER-SCOTIA COLLEGE at Concord, North Carolina, was founded in 1867 to educate newly freed slaves. It opened in a one room building with one teacher and ten students and offered elementary and secondary work to prepare black women for teaching and social work. In 1954 it started admitting students without regard to race or sex. LOCATION: Urban campus in large town, 20 miles from Charlotte. DEGREES OFFERED: BA, BS. ANNUAL EXPENSES: Tuition and fees $4,000. Room and board $2,487. Books and supplies $700. Other expenses $1,000. FALL TERM APPLICATIONS: $10 fee, may be waived for applicants with need. No closing date. Applicants notified on a rolling basis beginning on or about January 25. Interview recommended. Deferred admission available. CONTACT: Office of Enrollment Management, Barber-Scotia College, 145 Cabarrus Avenue West, Concord, NC 28025 (704) 786-5171 Ext. 237.

BENEDICT COLLEGE at Columbia, South Carolina was founded in 1870 by the Baptist church and remains a strongly church related institution. LOCATION: Urban campus in small city, 120 miles from Charleston. DEGREES OFFERED: BA, BS. ANNUAL EXPENSES: Tuition and fees $4,751. Room and board $2,418. Books and supplies $600. Other expenses $750. FALL TERM APPLICATIONS: $10 fee, may be waived for applicants with need. No closing date. Applicants notified on a rolling basis. Must reply within 4 weeks. Deferred admission available. CONTACT: Ms. Virginia McKee, Director Admissions and Records, Benedict College, Harden and Blanding Streets, Columbia, SC 29204 (803) 253-5143.

BENNETT COLLEGE at Greensboro, North Carolina, was founded in 1873 by the Freedmen's Aid Society and the Southern Education Society of the Methodist Episcopal church. Still church related but with private support, this women's college offers the bachelor's degree and provides liberal arts and teacher education curricula. LOCATION: Urban campus in small city, 295 miles south of Washington, DC. DEGREES OFFERED: AA, BA, BS. ANNUAL EXPENSES: Tuition and fees $5,230. Room and board $2,250. Books and supplies $600. Other expenses $1,000. FALL TERM APPLICATIONS: $20 fee, may be waived for applicants with need. Closing date August 1. Priority given to applications received by July 1. Applicants notified on a rolling basis. Must reply within 4 weeks. Interview recommended for borderline applicants. Deferred admission available. CONTACT: Susan Gibson, Director of Admissions, Bennett College, 900 East Washington Street, Greensboro, NC 27401-3239 (919) 273-4431.

BETHUNE-COOKMAN COLLEGE at Daytona Beach, Florida, was founded by a merger in 1923 of two Florida institutions: Cookman Institute of Jacksonville, founded in 1872 by Rev. D. S. B. Darnell, and the Daytona Normal and Industrial Institute for Negro Girls of Daytona Beach, founded in 1904 by Mary McLeod Bethune. The school is private, coeducational, and strongly church related. LOCATION: Urban campus in small city, 60 miles from Orlando. DEGREES OFFERED: BA, BS, MS. ANNUAL EXPENSES: Tuition and fees $4,835. Room and board $3,172. Books and supplies $405. Other expenses $1,405. FALL TERM APPLICATIONS: $25 fee. Closing date July 30. Priority given to applications received by June 1. Applicants notified on a rolling basis beginning on or about January 3. Must reply by August 15 or within 2 weeks if notified thereafter. Interview required for music applicants. Essay required. Deferred and early admission available. SAT/ACT recommended.

CONTACT: Dr. Roberto Barragan, Jr., Director of Admissions, Bethune-Cookman College, 640 Second Avenue, Daytona Beach, FL 32115 (904) 238-3803.

BLUEFIELD STATE COLLEGE at Bluefield, West Virginia, was founded in 1895. Its student body and faculty were predominantly black until about 1950. LOCATION: Urban campus in large town, 100 miles from Charleston, West Virginia. DEGREES OFFERED: AS, BA, BS. ANNUAL EXPENSES: Tuition and fees $1,316; $1,870 additional for out-of-state students. Books and supplies $800. Other expenses $900. FALL TERM APPLICATIONS: No fee. No closing date. Applicants notified on a rolling basis beginning on or about December 1. Deferred and early admission available. CONTACT: Mr. John C. Cardwell, Director of Admissions, Bluefield State College, Rock Street, Bluefield, WV 24701 (304) 327-4065.

BOWIE STATE UNIVERSITY at Bowie, Maryland, was founded in 1867 under the auspices of the Quakers as the Colored Normal School in Baltimore. It is currently state supported and coeducational. During the 1960s changes occurred in the composition of the student body, and the proportion of white students increased. LOCATION: Suburban campus in large town, 25 miles from Baltimore, 17 miles from Washington, DC. DEGREES OFFERED: BA, BS, BFA, MA, MS, MEd. ANNUAL EXPENSES: Tuition and fees $2,254; $1,925 additional for out-of-state students. Room and board $3,427. Books and supplies $450. Other expenses $900. FALL TERM APPLICATIONS: $10 fee, may be waived for applicants with need. Closing date April 1. Applicants notified on a rolling basis. Must reply by June 1 or within 7 days if notified

thereafter. Interview recommended. Audition recommended
for music education applicants. Portfolio recommended for
art applicants. Deferred and early admission available.
CONTACT: Mr. Lawrence Waters, Director of Admissions,
Records and Registration, Bowie State University, Jericho
Park Road, Bowie, MD 20715 (301) 464-6570.

CENTRAL STATE UNIVERSITY at Wilberforce, Ohio,
came into being in 1887. LOCATION: Rural campus in rural
community, 18 miles northeast of Dayton. DEGREES
OFFERED: AAS, BA, BS. ANNUAL EXPENSES: Tuition and
fees $2,247; $2,541 additional for out-of-state students.
Room and board $3,753. Other expenses $300. FALL TERM
APPLICATIONS: $15 fee, may be waived for applicants with
need. Closing date August 1; Applicants notified on a rolling
basis. Interview recommended. Deferred and early admission
available. ACT required for placement. Score report by
September 1. CONTACT: Mr. Robert E. Johnson, Director
of Admission and Enrollment Management, Central State
University, Brush Row Road, Wilberforce, OH 45384
(513) 376-6478.

CHEYNEY UNIVERSITY at Cheyney, Pennsylvania,
was founded in 1837 in Philadelphia through a bequest made
by Richard Humphreys, a Quaker philanthropist. It began
as a farm school before the Civil War, and then successively
became an evening school for apprentices, a high school for
training teachers, a teachers college, a state college, and
finally, a university. LOCATION: Rural campus in rural
community, 25 miles from Philadelphia. DEGREES OFFERED:
BA, BS, MA, MS. ANNUAL EXPENSES: Tuition and fees
$2,488; $2,034 additional for out-of-state students. Room

and board $2,956. Books and supplies $350. Other expenses $1,000. FALL TERM APPLICATIONS: $20 fee. May be waived for applicants with need. No closing date. Priority given to applications received by June 30. SAT score report by June 30. Applicants notified on a rolling basis beginning on or about January 1. Must reply within 4 weeks. Interview recommended. Essay recommended. CONTACT: Mr. Earl Acker, Director of Admissions, Cheyney University, Cheyney and Creek Roads, Cheyney, PA 19319 (215) 399-2275.

CLAFLIN COLLEGE at Orangeburg, South Carolina, was founded in 1869 and named in honor of Leo Claflin— a prominent Methodist of Boston—and his son William Claflin—a governor of Massachusetts—who were both instrumental in buying the property for the original site. Admission requirements for the first prospective students were good moral character and a conscientious desire to learn. LOCATION: Urban campus in large town, 40 miles from Columbia. DEGREES OFFERED: BA, BS. ANNUAL EXPENSES: Tuition and fees $4,018. Room and board $1,980. Books and supplies $350. Other expenses $500. FALL TERM APPLICATIONS: $10 fee, may be waived for applicants with need. No closing date. Priority given to applications received by July 30. Applicants notified on a rolling basis. Must reply within 6 weeks. SAT score report by September 1. CONTACT: Mr. George F. Lee, Director of Admission and Records, Claflin College, 700 College Avenue NE, Orangeburg, SC 29115 (803) 534-2710.

COAHOMA JUNIOR COLLEGE at Clarksdale, Mississippi, was founded in 1924. LOCATION: Rural community. DEGREES OFFERED: AA, AAS. ANNUAL EXPENSES: Tuition and fees $700; $400 additional for out-of-district students,

$1,400 additional for out-of-state students. Room and board
$1,897. Books and supplies $500. Other expenses $500. FALL
TERM APPLICATIONS: High school record most important for
admission to degree programs. Open admissions to vocational·
programs. CONTACT: Rita S. Hanfor, Director of Admissions,
Coahoma Junior College, Route 1, Box 616, Clarksdale, MS
38614 (601) 627-2571, Ext. 154.

COPPIN STATE COLLEGE at Baltimore, Maryland, was
founded in 1900 by the Baltimore school board. The school
began as a one-year training class for the preparation of black
elementary school teachers. It shared facilities with the
Colored Douglass High and Training School. By 1926
Coppin's one-year training class had expanded into a three-
year program and had become a separate institution with its
own principal. The institution was named Coppin Normal
School in honor of Fanny M. Jackson Coppin, a former slave,
who had become one of the first black women in the United
States to receive a college degree and who had introduced
teacher training programs into the educational system of
Philadelphia. The school features such unusual majors as
teacher education for exceptional children and training for
work with disadvantaged youth. LOCATION: Urban campus
in very large city, 50 miles from Washington, DC. DEGREES
OFFERED: BA, BS, MA, MS. ANNUAL EXPENSES. Tuition
and fees $2,241; $1,764 additional for out-of-state students.
Books and supplies $600. Other expenses $1,549. FALL TERM
APPLICATIONS: $15 fee, may be waived for applicants with
need. Closing date July 15. Applicants notified on a rolling
basis. Deferred and early admission available. CONTACT:
Mr. Allen Mosley, Director of Admissions, Coppin State
College, 2500 West North Avenue, Baltimore, MD 21216
(301) 383-5990.

DELAWARE STATE COLLEGE at Dover was founded in 1891 when the Delaware General Assembly passed "an Act to establish and maintain a college for the education of colored students in Agriculture and Mechanic Arts." The school became fully integrated after 1971. LOCATION: Suburban campus in large town. DEGREES OFFERED: BA, BS, MA, MS, MBA. ANNUAL EXPENSES: Tuition and fees $1,455; $1,875 additional for out-of-state students. Room and board $2,550. Books and supplies $400. Other expenses $1,250. FALL TERM APPLICATIONS: $10 fee. Closing date July 30. Priority given to applications received by June 1. Applicants notified on a rolling basis. Must reply by May 15. Interview recommended for nursing, some academically weak applicants. Deferred and early admission available. SAT score report by August 15. CONTACT: Mr. Jethro C. Williams, Director of Admissions, Delaware State College, 1200 N. Dupont Highway, Dover, DE 19901 (302) 739-4917.

DILLARD UNIVERSITY in New Orleans, Louisiana, was founded in 1869. In 1935 the university, which was named in honor of James Hardy Dillard, a white man who distinguished himself in the education of blacks in the South, began instruction. LOCATION: Urban campus in very large city. DEGREES OFFERED: BA, BS. ANNUAL EXPENSES: Tuition and fees $5,500. Room and board $3,250. Books and supplies $500. Other expenses $875. FALL TERM APPLICATIONS: $10 fee, may be waived for applicants with need. Closing date May 15. Priority given to applications received by April 15. Applicants notified on a rolling basis. Must reply within 2 weeks. Interview recommended, essay required. Deferred and early admission available. CONTACT: Mrs. Vernese B. O'Neal, Director of Admissions, Dillard University, 2601 Gentilly Boulevard, New Orleans, LA 70122-3097 (504) 283-8822.

EDWARD WATERS COLLEGE at Jacksonville, Florida, was founded in 1866 at Live Oak, Florida, under the auspices of the African Methodist Episcopal church. It was the first institution of higher learning for blacks in Florida and was originally intended to provide an educated ministry, beginning with the first primary grade and continuing through the higher grades. In 1934 the elementary school was discontinued, and in 1952 the high school programs were terminated. In 1955 the school became a junior college, and in 1958 it finally became a four-year college. LOCATION: Urban campus in very large city, 150 miles from Orlando. DEGREES OFFERED: BA, BS. ANNUAL EXPENSES: Tuition and fees $3,866. Room and board $3,850. Books and supplies $400. Other expenses $750. FALL TERM APPLICATIONS: Open admissions. CONTACT: Jerome Goodwin, Director of Admissions, Edward Waters College, 1658 Kings Road, Jacksonville, FL 32209 (904) 355-3030.

ELIZABETH CITY STATE UNIVERSITY at Elizabeth City, North Carolina, was founded in 1891 as the State Colored Normal School. LOCATION: Rural campus in large town, 50 miles south of Norfolk and Portsmouth, Virginia. DEGREES OFFERED: BA, BS. ANNUAL EXPENSES: Tuition and fees $1,077; $4,029 additional for out of state students. Room and board $2,464. Books and supplies $300. Other expenses $810. FALL TERM APPLICATIONS: $15 fee. No closing date. Priority given to applications received by August 15. Applicants notified on a rolling basis. Must reply as soon as possible. Deferred admission available. CONTACT: Office of Admissions, Elizabeth City State University, Parkview Drive, Elizabeth City, NC 27909 (919) 335-3305.

FAYETTEVILLE STATE UNIVERSITY at Fayetteville, North Carolina, was founded in 1877 by the General Assembly of North Carolina under the bill known as the Act to Establish Normal Schools. Prior to 1960 the only major offered was in elementary education. In 1959, however, the general assembly revised the university's charter and authorized expansion of the curriculum to include a major in secondary education. The university now offers sixteen majors and a cooperative program with North Carolina State University which adds ten additional majors. Fayetteville State graduated its first four year class in 1939 and its first white student in 1964. LOCATION: Urban campus in small city, 60 miles from Raleigh. Degrees offered: AA, BA, BS, MA, MBA. ANNUAL EXPENSES: Tuition and fees $981; $4,573 additional for out-of-state students. Room and board $2,150. Books and supplies $325. Other expenses $500. FALL TERM APPLICATIONS: High school diploma required. CONTACT: Charles A. Darlington, Director of Admissions, Fayetteville State University, 1200 Murchison Road, Fayetteville, NC 28301-4298 (919) 486-1371.

FISK UNIVERSITY at Nashville, Tennessee, was founded in 1866. Known at the time it opened its doors as Fisk Free School, its founders, E. M. Cravath and E. P. Smith of the American Missionary Association and John Ogden of the Freedmen's Bureau proposed to offer a free school based upon a "broad Christian foundation." The founders intended to satisfy the desperate need for qualified black teachers and hoped that Fisk would ultimately become a first class college that would give black youth the same educational opportunities enjoyed by whites. LOCATION: Urban campus in very

large city, 216 miles from Memphis, 225 miles from Atlanta.
DEGREES OFFERED: BA, BFA, MA. ANNUAL EXPENSES:
Tuition and fees $5,520. Room and board $3,355. Books
and supplies $600. Other expenses $2,583. FALL TERM
APPLICATIONS: $15 fee, may be waived for applicants with
need. No closing date. Priority given to applications received
by March 15. Applicants notified on a rolling basis. Must
reply within 30 days. Audition recommended for music
applicants. Essay recommended. Deferred and early
admission available. December 1 closing date for early
admission applicants. CONTACT: Harrison F. DeShields, Jr.,
Director of Admissions and Records, Fisk University, 17th
Avenue North, Nashville, TN 37203 (615) 329-8665.

**FLORIDA AGRICULTURAL AND MECHANICAL (A&M)
UNIVERSITY** at Tallahassee, Florida, was founded in 1887.
LOCATION: Urban campus in small city, 169 miles from
Jacksonville. DEGREES OFFERED: AA, BA, BS, BArch, MA,
MS, MBA, MEd, PhD, PharmD. ANNUAL EXPENSES:
Tuition and fees $1,582; 4,138 additional for out-of-state stu-
dents. Room and board $2,652. Books and supplies $315.
Other expenses $1,050. FALL TERM APPLICATIONS: $15 fee.
Closing date July 15. Priority given to applications received
by May 1. Applicants notified on a rolling basis. Interview
recommended for nursing, physical therapy, architecture,
pharmacy, engineering applicants. Audition required for
music applicants. Portfolio required for architecture applicants. Essay required for borderline applicants. Deferred and
early admission available. CONTACT: Barbara Cox, Director
of Admissions/Deputy Registrar, Florida A&M University,
Tallahassee, FL 32307 (904) 599-3796.

FLORIDA MEMORIAL COLLEGE at Miami, Florida, was founded in 1892 by the Baptists and is still a church related organization. The college graduated its first four year class in 1945. In 1963 its charter was amended to open the institution to students of all races. LOCATION: Suburban campus in very large city, located 15 miles from downtown Miami. DEGREES OFFERED: BA, BS. ANNUAL EXPENSES: Tuition and fees $4,550. Room and board $2,800. Books and supplies $500. Other expenses $810. FALL TERM APPLICATIONS: $15 fee, may be waived for applicants with need. Closing date July 1. Priority given to applications received by April 1. Applicants notified on a rolling basis. Must reply by August 1. Interview recommended; essay required. Deferred admission available. CONTACT: Peggy Kelly, Director of Admissions, Florida Memorial College, 15800 Northwest 42 Avenue, Miami, FL 33054 (305) 623-4145.

FORT VALLEY STATE COLLEGE at Fort Valley, Georgia, was founded in 1895. LOCATION: Rural campus in small town, 30 miles from Macon. DEGREES OFFERED: AA, AS, BA, BS, MA, MS. ANNUAL EXPENSES: Tuition and fees $1,722; $1,341 additional for out-of-state students. Room and board $2,370. Books and supplies $600. Other expenses $1,320. FALL TERM APPLICATIONS: No fee. Closing date August 25. Applicants notified on a rolling basis beginning on or about February 1. Must reply within 4 weeks. Audition recommended for music education applicants. Early admission available. CONTACT: Delia W. Taylor, Director of Admissions and Recruitment, Fort Valley State College, P.O. Box 4531 EVSC, State College Drive, Fort Valley, GA 31030 (912) 825-6307.

GRAMBLING COLLEGE at Grambling, Louisiana, was founded in 1901. The original purpose of the institution was to teach Afro-Americans how to make a living by improving methods of farming. All students were accepted, as long as they were willing to work. LOCATION: Rural campus in small town, 35 miles from Monroe, 70 miles from Shreveport. DEGREES OFFERED: AA, AS, BA, BS, MA, MS, MBA, EdD. ANNUAL EXPENSES: Tuition and fees $1,778; $1,550 additional for out of state students. Room and board $2,636. Books and supplies $500. Other expenses $930. FALL TERM APPLICATIONS: $5 fee. Closing date July 15. Applicants notified on a rolling basis. Audition recommended for music applicants. Deferred and early admission available. CONTACT: Miss Karen Lewis, Director of Admissions, Grambling College, 100 Main Street Box 584, Grambling, LA 71245 (318) 274-2435.

HAMPTON UNIVERSITY at Hampton, Virginia, was founded in 1868 by Samuel Chapman Armstrong, a twenty-seven-year-old brevet brigadier general who commanded the U.S. Eighth and Ninth black troops during the Civil War. One of Hampton's most eminent graduates was Booker T. Washington, founder of Tuskegee Institute. In his autobiography, *Up From Slavery*, Washington describes his life as a Hampton student and his work there after his graduation. LOCATION: Urban campus in small city, 10 miles from Norfolk. DEGREES OFFERED: BA, BS, BArch, MA, MS, MBA. ANNUAL EXPENSES: Tuition and fees $7,006. Room and board $3,120. Books and supplies $600. Other expenses $500. FALL TERM APPLICATIONS: $10 fee. Closing date February 15. Applicants notified on or about March 1. Must reply by April 1. Audition required for music applicants. Deferred and early admission available. CONTACT: Dr. Ollie M. Bowman, Dean of Admissions, Hampton University, Hampton, VA 23668 (804) 727-5328.

HOWARD UNIVERSITY at Washington, DC, was founded in 1867. Founded on its present site, then a farm, the university was originally intended to meet the needs of newly freed slaves. It began with two academic departments, four students, and a faculty of one. Howard's complete role, however, has not been restricted solely to the education of African-Americans. Throughout its history, it has accepted students who were not black. Indeed, among its white graduates was the first woman physician in the District of Columbia. Its black graduates, however, in both number and distinction, reflect the significant place that the university has occupied in African-American academic and public life. For example, about half of the nation's black physicians, surgeons, and dentists are Howard graduates. About 25 percent of all black lawyers and more than 50 percent of Afro-American engineers and architects are graduates of Howard. LOCATION: Urban campus in very large city, located in northwest section of city. DEGREES OFFERED: BA, BS, BFA, BArch, MA, MS, MBA, MFA, MEd, PhD, EdD, DMD, MD, PharmD, JD. ANNUAL EXPENSES: Tuition and fees $6,941. Room and board $3,600. Books and supplies $555. Other expenses $2,250. FALL TERM APPLICATIONS: $25 fee. Closing date April 1. Applicants notified on a rolling basis. Must reply within 4 weeks. Interview recommended for pharmacy and pharmacological sciences. Audition required for music, drama applicants. Portfolio required for art applicants. Essay recommended. Deferred and early admission available.

CONTACT: Emmet R. Griffin, Director of Admissions, Howard University, 2400 Sixth Street NW, Washington, DC 20059 (202) 806-2752.

HUSTON-TILLOTSON COLLEGE at Austin, Texas, was founded in 1876. One of its buildings, Allen Hall, constructed in 1881, is thought to be the first building erected in the state of Texas and west of the Mississippi River for the higher education of African-Americans. LOCATION: Urban campus in large city, 78 miles north of San Antonio. DEGREES OFFERED: BA, BS. ANNUAL EXPENSES: Tuition and fees $4,440. Room and board $3,290. Books and supplies $490. Other expenses $980. FALL TERM APPLICATIONS: $15 fee. No closing date. Priority given to applications received by March 1. Applicants notified on a rolling basis beginning on or about May 1. Interview recommended. Audition recommended. Deferred admission available. CONTACT: Donnie J. Scott, Director of Admissions, Huston-Tillotson College, 1820 East Eighth Street, Austin, TX 78702 (512) 476-7421.

JACKSON STATE COLLEGE at Jackson, Mississippi, was founded in 1877. It opened with twenty students to educate teachers and preachers. LOCATION: Urban campus in large city, 210 miles southwest of Memphis. DEGREES OFFERED: BA, BS, MA, MS, MBA, MEd, PhD, EdD. ANNUAL EXPENSES: Tuition and fees $2,028, $1,462 additional for out-of-state students. Room and board $2,610. Books and supplies $500. Other expenses $1,018. FALL TERM APPLICATIONS: No fee. Closing date August 15. Applicants notified on a rolling basis beginning on or about January 1. Audition recommended for music applicants. Deferred and early admission available. CONTACT: Barbara Luckett,

Director of Admissions and Recruitment, Jackson State University, 1400 J.R. Lynch Street, Jackson, MS 39217 (601) 968-2100.

JARVIS CHRISTIAN COLLEGE at Hawkins, Texas, was founded in 1912 by the Disciples of Christ and is still affiliated with that church. In a circumstance that may be unique among schools, oil was discovered on Jarvis' property in 1941 and by the 1970s, nineteen wells were operating. One-fourth of the net income from oil is allocated to the endowment fund, one-fourth to capital reserves, and one-half to operating costs. LOCATION: Rural campus in rural community, 100 miles east of Dallas, 100 miles west of Shreveport, Louisiana. DEGREES OFFERED: BA, BS. ANNUAL EXPENSES: Tuition and fees $4,015. Room and board $2,999. Books and supplies $300. Other expenses $900. FALL TERM APPLICATIONS: $15 fee. No closing date. Applicants notified on a rolling basis beginning on or about January 25. Interview recommended. Essay required. Deferred and early admission available. CONTACT: Linda Rutherford, Director of Recruitment and Admissions, Jarvis Christian College, P.O. Drawer G, Hawkins, TX 75765 (903) 769-2174 ext. 233.

JOHNSON C. SMITH UNIVERSITY at Charlotte, North Carolina, was founded in 1867 by the Presbyterian church and is still affiliated with it. In 1867 Rev. SC. Alexander and WL. Miller recognized the need for a school for African-Americans in North Carolina. At a meeting of the Catawba Presbytery in the old Charlotte Presbyterian Church in Charlotte, the movement for a school for boys and young men was formally inaugurated. Alexander and Miller were elected teachers. The main purpose of the school was to train men for the ministry, for catechists, and for teaching. In 1932, the institution became coeducational. Until 1941 women were admitted to the senior college division only, but beginning with the school year 1941-42, they were also admitted to the freshman class. LOCATION: Urban campus in large city. DEGREES OFFERED: BA, BS. ANNUAL EXPENSES: Tuition and fees $5,671. Room and board $2,158. Books and supplies $400. Other expenses $1,560. FALL TERM APPLICATIONS: $20 fee may be waived, no closing date. Priority given to applications received by August 1. Applicants notified on a rolling basis beginning on or about October 1. Interview and essay recommended. Deferred and early admission available. CONTACT: Ms. Judith Cowan, Director of Admissions, Johnson C. Smith University, 100 Beatties Ford Road, Charlotte, NC 28216-5398 (704) 378-1010.

KENTUCKY STATE UNIVERSITY at Frankfort, Kentucky, was founded in 1886 by an act of the Kentucky General Assembly as the Kentucky State Normal School for Colored Persons. LOCATION: Urban campus in large town, 50 miles east of Louisville, 25 miles west of Lexington. DEGREES OFFERED: AA, AS, BA, BS. ANNUAL EXPENSES: Tuition and fees $1,440; $2,680 additional for out-of-state students. Room and board $2,682. Books and supplies $510. Other expenses $800. FALL TERM APPLICATIONS: $5 fee. No closing date. Applicants notified on a rolling basis. Interview recommended for nursing and Whitney M. Young, Jr., College of Leadership Studies applicants. Portfolio recommended for art applicants. Essay required for Whitney M. Young, Jr. College of Leadership Studies applicants. Early admission available. CONTACT: Tava Clay, Associate Director of Admissions, Kentucky State University, East Main Street, Frankfort, KY 40601 (502) 227-6813.

KNOXVILLE COLLEGE at Knoxville, Tennessee, was founded in 1875 by Presbyterian missionaries to provide education for freedmen and their children after the Civil War. Programs ranged from primary through high school levels until the 1890s when collegiate programs became available. LOCATION: Urban campus in small city, 177 miles northeast of Nashville. DEGREES OFFERED: AA, BA, BS. ANNUAL EXPENSES: Tuition and fees $5,270. Room and board $3,500. Books and supplies $600. Other expenses $2,050. FALL TERM APPLICATIONS: $15 fee, may be waived for applicants with need. No closing date. Applicants notified on a rolling basis beginning on or about January 2. Audition required for music applicants. Essay recommended. Deferred admission available. CONTACT: Robert Thomas, Director of Admissions, Knoxville College, 901 College Street, Knoxville, TN 37921 (615) 524-6568.

LANE COLLEGE at Jackson, Tennessee, was founded by Isaac Lane in 1882 as the Christian Methodist High School. In 1887 Rev. TF. Saunders, a member of the Memphis Conference of the Methodist Episcopal church was appointed the first president and made numerous contributions to the institute. It was during this period that the need for a college department was felt. This department was organized in 1896, and the name of the school was changed. LOCATION: Suburban campus in small city. DEGREES OFFERED: BA, BS. ANNUAL EXPENSES: Tuition and fees $4,357. Room and board $2,473. Books and supplies $400. Other expenses $900. FALL TERM APPLICATIONS: No fee. Closing date August 1. Priority given to applications received by July 15. Applicants notified on a rolling basis. CONTACT: Ruth Maddox, Director of Admissions, Lane College, 545 Lane Avenue, Jackson, TN 38301 (901) 426-7500.

LANGSTON UNIVERSITY at Langston, Oklahoma, was established in 1897 by the territorial legislature. The school was first chartered as the Colored Agricultural and Normal University, but it was commonly known as Langston after the name of the village where it was located. LOCATION: Rural campus in rural community, 40 miles northeast of Oklahoma City. DEGREES OFFERED: AA, AS, BA, BS, MEd. ANNUAL EXPENSES: Tuition and fees $1,318; $1,920 additional for out-of-state students. Room and board $2,420. Books and supplies $425. FALL TERM APPLICATIONS: No fee. No closing date. Priority given to applications received by March 1. Applicants notified on a rolling basis. Audition recommended for music applicants. Early admission available. CONTACT: Jo Ann Clark, Director of Admissions, Langston University, P.O. Box 838, Langston, OK 73050 (405) 466-2231.

LAWSON STATE COMMUNITY COLLEGE at Birmingham, Alabama, was founded in 1963 as a public institution. LOCATION: Suburban campus in large city, 10 miles southwest of Birmingham. DEGREES OFFERED: AA, AS, AAS. ANNUAL EXPENSES: Tuition and fees $984; $720 additional for out-of-district students, $606 additional for out-of-state students. Books and supplies $400. Other expenses $700. FALL TERM APPLICATIONS: No fee. No closing date. Applicants notified on a rolling basis. Deferred and early admission available. CONTACT: Myra P. Davis, Coordinator of Admissions and Records, Lawson State Community College, 3060 Wilson Road SW, Birmingham, AL 35221-1717 (205) 925-2515 ext. 309.

LEMOYNE-OWEN COLLEGE at Memphis, Tennessee, was founded in 1870. LOCATION: Urban campus in very large city, 200 miles from Nashville. DEGREES OFFERED: BA, BS.

ANNUAL EXPENSES: Tuition and fees $3,750. Books and supplies $400. Other expenses $900. FALL TERM APPLICATIONS: $25 fee, may be waived for applicants with need. Closing date June 15. Priority given to applications received by May 15. Applicants notified on a rolling basis. Must reply within 2 weeks. Interview required. Essay required. Deferred admission available. CONTACT: Marie Millan, Director of Admissions, LeMoyne-Owen College, 807 Walker Avenue, Memphis, TN 38126 (901) 942-7302.

LINCOLN UNIVERSITY at Jefferson City, Missouri, was founded in 1866. It was the only state supported college for African-Americans under segregation. LOCATION: Suburban campus in large town, 132 miles from St. Louis, 152 miles from Kansas City. DEGREES OFFERED: AA, AAS, BA, BS, MA, MBA, MEd. ANNUAL EXPENSES: Tuition and fees $1,498; $1,478 additional for out-of-of-state students. Room and board $2,728. Books and supplies $480. Other expenses $1,496. FALL TERM APPLICATIONS: $17 fee. No closing date. Priority given to applications received by July 15. Applicants notified on a rolling basis. Must reply as soon as possible. Audition required for music education applicants. Deferred admission available. CONTACT: Charles E. Glasper, Director of Admissions, Lincoln University, 820 Chestnut, Jefferson City, MO 65101 (314) 681-5000.

LINCOLN UNIVERSITY of Pennsylvania was founded in 1854 "for the scientific, classical, and theological education of colored youth of the male sex." Since the turn of the century the number of Lincoln alumni to have undertaken graduate study in the various professions—most notably medicine, dentistry, law, and education—has increased to include more than 50 percent of Lincoln's graduates. By the end of the 1950s Lincoln had some white students and was coeducational. LOCATION: Rural campus in rural community, 45 miles from Philadelphia. DEGREES OFFERED: BA, BS, MA, MS. ANNUAL EXPENSES: Tuition and fees $2,960; $1,420 additional for out-of-state students. Room and board $2,800. Books and supplies $485. Other expenses $1,016. FALL TERM APPLICATIONS: $10 fee, may be waived for students with need. No closing date. Applicants notified on a rolling basis. Must reply within 2 weeks. Interview recommended for borderline applicants. Essay required. Deferred and early admission available. CONTACT: Jimmy Arrington, Director of Admissions, Lincoln University, Lincoln Hall, Lincoln University, PA 19352-0999 (215) 932-8300.

LIVINGSTONE COLLEGE at Salisbury, North Carolina, was founded in 1879 and was named in honor of David Livingstone, the explorer. The college offers a summer program in communications skills for junior and senior high school students who need strengthening in this area before attempting college work. LOCATION: Urban campus in large town, 44 miles from Charlotte. DEGREES OFFERED: BA, BS. ANNUAL EXPENSES: Tuition and fees $3,784. Room and board $2,494. Books and supplies $675. Other expenses $750. FALL TERM APPLICATIONS: $10 fee, may be waived for applicants with need. No closing date. Applicants notified on a rolling basis beginning on or about May 15. Must reply within 2 weeks. Interview recommended for academically weak applicants. Audition required for music applicants. SAT or ACT score report due by August 15. CONTACT: Grady Deese, Director of Admissions, Livingstone College, 701 West Monroe Street, Salisbury, NC 28144 (704) 638-5500.

MARY HOLMES COLLEGE at West Point, Mississippi, was founded in 1892. It opened with an enrollment of 168 as a seminary for training Afro-American girls in domestic arts and Christian service. Destroyed by fire two years after its founding, the school reopened in 1897 on a tract of land donated by citizens of the community. LOCATION: Rural campus in large town, 75 miles from Tuscaloosa, Alabama. DEGREES OFFERED: AA, AS. ANNUAL EXPENSES: Tuition and fees $4,100. Room and board $3,800. Books and supplies $700. Other expenses $700. FALL TERM APPLICATIONS: No fee. No closing date. Priority given to applications received by July 31. Applicants notified on a rolling basis. Interview recommended. Essay recommended. Deferred admission available. CONTACT: James Stewart, Enrollment Marketing Manager, Mary Holmes College, P.O. Drawer 1257, Highway 50 West, West Point, MS 39773-1257 (601) 494-6820 ext 139.

MILES COLLEGE at Fairfield, Alabama, was founded in 1907. The college is concerned with the welfare of people, especially the black community of nearby Birmingham. Miles tries to assist the capable student, regardless of financial circumstances. To this end, it has a strong financial-aid program. LOCATION: Campus in large town, 6 miles from downtown Birmingham. DEGREES OFFERED: BA, BS. ANNUAL EXPENSES: Tuition and fees $3,760. Room and board $2,300. Books and Supplies $400. Other expenses $1,000. FALL TERM APPLICATIONS: $25 fee, may be waived for applicants with need. Closing date July 15. Applicants notified on a rolling basis. Must reply by August 1. CONTACT: Gloria Ann W. Beverly, Director of Admissions, Miles College, 5500 Myron-Massey Boulevard, Fairfield, AL 35064 (205) 923-2771.

MOREHOUSE COLLEGE at Atlanta, Georgia, is an independent college for men, strongly oriented toward teacher education, and its religious origins still exert some influence. From a school that began with a student body of thirty-seven former slaves and three faculty members who met in the basement of Springfield Baptist Church in Augusta, Morehouse has grown to a fully accredited liberal arts college and leads all predominantly black four-year colleges in the percentage of alumni who have received doctorates. Distinguished graduates include Dr. Martin Luther King, Jr., Spike Lee, and Julian Bond. LOCATION: Urban campus in very large city, 2 miles from downtown. DEGREES OFFERED: BA, BS. ANNUAL EXPENSES: Tuition and fees $6,692. Room and board $4,734. Books and supplies $500. Other expenses $2,500. FALL TERM APPLICATIONS: $35 fee, may be waived for applicants with need. Closing date February 15. Priority given to applications received by January 15. Applicants notified on or about April 1. Must reply by May 1. Interview recommended. Essay required. Deferred and early admission available. Early action applicants must complete process by October 15. CONTACT: Sterling H. Hudson III, Director of Admissions, Morehouse College, 830 Westview Drive SW, Atlanta, GA 30314 (404) 681-2800.

MORGAN STATE UNIVERSITY at Baltimore, Maryland, graduates have an outstanding record in public and community service. For example, four of the five Afro-American Maryland state senators in 1975 were Morgan graduates, and five of the fourteen African-Americans in the Maryland House of Delegates were either graduates or had attended the university. LOCATION: Urban campus in very large city, 45 miles northeast of Washington, DC, 100 miles south of Philadelphia. DEGREES OFFERED: BA, BS, MA, MS, MBA,

EdD. ANNUAL EXPENSES: Tuition and fees $2,438; $2,068 additional for out-of-state students. Room and board $4,640. Books and supplies $800. Other expenses $1,500. FALL TERM APPLICATIONS: $20 fee, may be waived for applicants with need. No closing date. Priority given to applications received by April 15. Applicants notified on a rolling basis. Must reply by May 1 or within 4 weeks if notified thereafter. Interview recommended. Audition recommended for music applicants. Deferred and early admission available. CONTACT: Chelseia Harold-Miller, Director of Admissions and Recruitment, Morgan State University, Cold Spring Lane and Hillen Road, Baltimore, MD 21239 (410) 319-3000.

MORRIS BROWN COLLEGE at Atlanta, Georgia, was founded in 1881, a product of the self-help concept generated among African-Americans after slavery in an effort to educate their children. LOCATION: Urban campus in very large city, 2 miles from downtown Atlanta. DEGREES OFFERED: BA, BS. ANNUAL EXPENSES: Tuition and fees $7,032. Room and board $4,150. Books and supplies $600. Other expenses $650. FALL TERM APPLICATIONS: $20 fee, may be waived for applicants with need. No closing date. Priority given to applications received by June 30. Applicants notified on a rolling basis beginning on or about February 1. Must reply within 4 weeks. Essay recommended. Early admission available. CONTACT: Tyrone Fletcher, Director of Admissions, Morris Brown College, 643 Martin Luther King Jr. Drive NW, Atlanta, GA 30314 (404) 220-0270.

MORRIS COLLEGE at Sumter, South Carolina, was founded in 1908. The college pursues a policy of keeping its enrollment small, and the faculty makes a particular effort to spend as much time as possible with the students in informal surroundings. LOCATION: Urban campus in large town, 45 miles from Columbia. DEGREES OFFERED: BA, BS, BFA. ANNUAL EXPENSES: Tuition and fees $4,136. Room and board $2,434. Books and supplies $725. Other expenses $1,000. FALL TERM APPLICATIONS: $10 fee, may be waived for applicants with need. No closing date. Applicants notified on a rolling basis. CONTACT: Queen W. Spann, Director of Admission and Records, Morris College, 100 West College Street, Sumter, SC 29150-3599 (803) 775-9371 ext. 225.

NORFOLK STATE UNIVERSITY at Norfolk, Virginia. LOCATION: Urban campus in large city. DEGREES OFFERED: AS, BA, BS, MA, MS, MFA. ANNUAL EXPENSES: Tuition and fees $2,530, $3,230 additional for out-of-state students. Room and board $3,400. Books and supplies $550. Other expenses $300. FALL TERM APPLICATIONS: $15 fee, may be waived for applicants with need. No closing date. Priority given to applications received by June 1. Applicants notified on a rolling basis beginning on or about February 1. Interview recommended for nursing, electronics, engineering applicants. Audition recommended for music applicants. Portfolio recommended for art applicants. Deferred and early admission available. CONTACT: Dr. Frank W. Cool, Director of Admissions, Norfolk State University, 2401 Corprew Avenue, Norfolk, VA 25304 (804) 683-8396.

NORTH CAROLINA CENTRAL UNIVERSITY at Durham, North Carolina, was chartered in 1909 and opened in 1910. LOCATION: Urban campus in small city, 23 miles from Raleigh. DEGREES OFFERED: BA, BS, BArch, MA, MS, MBA, MEd, JD. ANNUAL EXPENSES: Tuition and fees $1,169;

$5,054 additional for out-of-state students. Room and board $2,915. Books and supplies $290. Other expenses $630. FALL TERM APPLICATIONS: $15 fee. Closing date August 1. Priority given to applications received by July 1. Applicants notified on a rolling basis. Must reply by June 1 for college housing. Audition required for music applicants. Early admission available. CONTACT: Nancy R. Rowland, Director of Admissions, North Carolina Central University, P.O. Box 19717, Durham, NC 27702 (919) 560-6298.

OAKWOOD COLLEGE at Huntsville, Alabama, was founded in 1896 by Seventh Day Adventists. LOCATION: Suburban campus in small city. DEGREES OFFERED: AA, AS, BA, BS. ANNUAL EXPENSES: Tuition and fees $6,216. Room and board $3,663. Books and supplies $600. Other expenses $1,500. FALL TERM APPLICATIONS: $15 fee, may be waived for applicants with need. No closing date. Applicants notified on a rolling basis. Essay recommended. Deferred admission available. CONTACT: Lovey Verdun, Assistant Director of Admissions and Records, Oakwood College, Oakwood Road, Huntsville, AL 35896 (205) 726-7000 ext. 7939.

PAINE COLLEGE at Augusta, Georgia, was founded in 1882. Since no public schools for Afro-Americans existed in that area, Paine provided secondary education as well as college work for its students. It was not until 1945, in the wake of the first public high school education for blacks in Augusta that Paine decided to discontinue its preparatory classes. LOCATION: Urban campus in large town, 74 miles from Columbia, South Carolina. DEGREES OFFERED: BA, BS. ANNUAL EXPENSES: Tuition and fees $5,468. Room and board $2,739. Books and supplies $400. Other expenses $485. FALL TERM APPLICATIONS: $10 fee. No closing date.

Applicants notified on a rolling basis. Interview recommended. Essay required. Audition required for music education applicants. Deferred and early admission available. CONTACT: Phyllis Wyatt-Woodruff, Director of Enrollment Management, Paine College, 1235 15th Street, Augusta, GA 30910-2799 (706) 821-8320.

PAUL QUINN COLLEGE at Waco, Texas, was founded in 1872 and had its beginning in a one room building in Austin, Texas, after a group of Methodist agreed on the need for a trade school to teach newly freed slaves blacksmithing, carpentry, tanning, saddlery and other skills to make them self sufficient. LOCATION: Urban campus in small city, 95 miles from Dallas. DEGREES OFFERED: BA, BS. ANNUAL EXPENSES: Tuition and fees $3,635. Room and board $2,975. Books and supplies $400. Other expenses $700. FALL TERM APPLICATIONS: No fee. No closing date. Applicants notified on a rolling basis. Deferred admission available. CONTACT: Marilyn Marshall, Director of Admission and Support Services, Paul Quinn College, 3837 Simpson Stuart Road, Dallas, TX 75241 (214) 376-1000.

PHILANDER SMITH COLLEGE at Little Rock, Arkansas, was founded in 1877 by the Methodist Episcopal church. LOCATION: Urban campus in small city; in downtown area. DEGREES OFFERED: BA, BS. ANNUAL EXPENSES: Tuition and fees $2,350. Room and board $2,300. Books and supplies $400. Other expenses $750. FALL TERM APPLICATIONS: $5 fee, may be waived for applicants with need. No closing date. Applicants notified on a rolling basis. Deferred admission available. CONTACT: Picola Smith, Director of Admissions and Records, Philander Smith College, 812 West 13th Street, Little Rock, AR 72202 (501) 375-9845.

PRAIRIE VIEW AGRICULTURAL AND MECHANICAL (A&M) UNIVERSITY at Prairie View, Texas, was founded in 1876, and today is part of the Texas A&M University system. Its 1,400 acre campus is a community in itself and has become an incorporated city. The college furnishes its own water, steam power, and sewage disposal. It also has its own telephone and telegraph system, security patrol, U.S. post office, college exchange store, and laboratory training school. LOCATION: Rural campus in small town, 45 miles northwest of Houston. DEGREES OFFERED: BA, BS, BFA, BArch, MA, MS, MBA MEd. ANNUAL EXPENSES: Tuition and fees $1,535; $4,140 additional for out-of-state students. Room and board $3,300. Books and supplies $533. FALL TERM APPLICATIONS: No fee. No closing date. Applicants notified on a rolling basis. Essay required for honors college applicants. Deferred and early admission available. CONTACT: Linda Berry, Director Admissions and Records, Prairie View A&M University, P.O. Box 2777, Prairie View, TX 77446 (409) 857-2626.

RUST COLLEGE at Holly Springs, Mississippi, was founded in 1866 and was named for Richard Rust, a white antislavery advocate. Over the years, Rust played a vital part in the educational system of Mississippi. First it taught ex-slaves how to read and write. Later, it offered them or their descendants agricultural and domestic science courses. Then, because of the limitations of public school training for Afro-American youth, Rust made it possible for many of these students to qualify for entrance into predominantly white colleges. Most of these students came from culturally deprived homes and communities. LOCATION: Rural campus in small town, 45 miles southeast of Memphis. DEGREES OFFERED: AS, BA, BS. ANNUAL EXPENSES: Tuition and fees $4,152. Room and

board $1,948. Books and supplies $225. Other expenses $150.
FALL TERM APPLICATIONS: $10 fee, may be waived for
applicants with need. No closing date. Applicants notified
on a rolling basis. Must reply by May 1 or within 2 weeks if
notified thereafter. Early admission available. CONTACT:
JoAnn Scott, Director of Admissions and Recruitment, Rust
College, 150 Rust Avenue, Holly Springs, MS 38635-2328
(601) 252-4661 ext. 4068.

SAINT AUGUSTINE'S COLLEGE at Raleigh, North
Carolina, was founded in 1867. LOCATION: Urban campus in
small city, approximately 170 miles from Charlotte. DEGREES
OFFERED: BA, BS. ANNUAL EXPENSES: Tuition and fees
$5,300. Room and board $3,400. Books and supplies $500.
Other expenses $550. FALL TERM APPLICATIONS: $10 fee.
Closing date August 1. Applicants notified on a rolling basis.
CONTACT: Wanzo F. Hendrix, Director of Admissions and
Retention, Saint Augustine's College, 1315 Oak Avenue,
Raleigh, NC 27610-2298 (919) 828-4451.

SAINT PAUL'S COLLEGE at Lawrenceville, Virginia, was
founded in 1888. LOCATION: Rural campus in small town,
80 miles from Richmond. DEGREES OFFERED: BA, BS.
ANNUAL EXPENSES: Tuition and fees $4,935. Room and
board $3,330. Books and supplies $450. Other expenses $674.
FALL TERM APPLICATIONS: $15 fee. No closing date.
Applicants notified on a rolling basis. Must reply by May 1 or
within 2 weeks if notified thereafter. Interview recommended.
Essay recommended. Deferred and early admission available.
CONTACT: L. R. Parker, Director of Admissions and
Recruitment, Saint Paul's College, 406 Windsor Avenue,
Lawrenceville, VA 23868 (804) 848-3984.

SAVANNAH STATE COLLEGE at Savannah, Georgia, was founded in 1890 as one of the departments of the state university but one expressly for the education and training of Afro-American students. It was originally called the Georgia State Industrial College for Colored Youth. From its beginnings with three faculty members, a principal, eight students, eighty-six acres of land, two buildings and a farm-house, Savannah State College has grown to be the largest predominantly African-American institution in the state. LOCATION: Urban campus in small city, adjacent to city limits. DEGREES OFFERED: AS, BA, BS. ANNUAL EXPENSES: Tuition and fees $1,686; $1,341 additional for out-of-state students. Room and board $2,205. Books and supplies $600. Other expenses $900. FALL TERM APPLICATIONS: $10 fee, may be waived for applicants with need. Closing date September 1. Applicants notified on a rolling basis beginning on or about March 1. Deferred and early admission available. CONTACT: Robert L. Ray, Director of Admissions and Records, Savannah State College, State College Branch, Savannah, GA 31404 (912) 356-2181.

SELMA UNIVERSITY at Selma, Alabama, was founded in 1878 by Baptists to train ministers and teachers. LOCATION: Urban campus in large town, 50 miles west of Montgomery. DEGREES OFFERED: AA, AS, AAS, BA, BS. ANNUAL EXPENSES: Tuition and fees $4,200. Room and board $3,700. Books and supplies: $200. Other expenses $600. FALL TERM APPLICATIONS: $10 fee. No closing date. Applicants notified on a rolling basis beginning on or about August 1. CONTACT: Raymond Brown, Director of Admissions and Records, Selma University, 1501 Lapsley Street, Selma, AL 36701 (205) 872-2533.

SHAW UNIVERSITY at Raleigh, North Carolina was founded in 1865. In its earliest days, Shaw maintained a medical school, one of the first for Afro-Americans, though now its programs emphasize the liberal arts and teacher education. Shaw has several unusual features. For example, although its student body remains mostly Afro-American, its faculty is both interracial and multicultural. More than 25 percent of the staff are natives of non-Western countries. Shaw also had one of the earliest black studies programs. LOCATION: Urban campus in small city. DEGREES OFFERED: AA, BA, BS. ANNUAL EXPENSES: Tuition and fees $4,894. Room and board $3,325. Books and supplies $850. Other expenses $1,000. FALL TERM APPLICATIONS: $25, may be waived for applicants with need. Closing date August 10. Applicants notified on a rolling basis. Must reply within 2 weeks. Essay recommended. CONTACT: Alfonza Carter, Director of Admissions, Shaw University, 118 East South Street, Raleigh, NC 27611 (919) 546-8220.

SHORTER COLLEGE at North Little Rock, Arkansas, was founded in 1886. LOCATION: Urban campus in small city, 1.5 miles from Little Rock. DEGREES OFFERED: AA, AS, AAS. ANNUAL EXPENSES: Tuition and fees $2,110. Room and board $2,200. Books and supplies $250. Other expenses $200. FALL TERM APPLICATIONS: $5 fee. Closing date August 31. Priority given to applications received by May 12. Applicants notified on a rolling basis. Must reply within one week. Interview recommended. Deferred and early admission available. Applicants notified of fall term admissions decision after taking entrance examination. CONTACT: Delores Voliber, Director of Admissions, Shorter College, 604 Locust Street, North Little Rock, AR 72114 (501) 374-6305.

SOUTH CAROLINA STATE COLLEGE at Orangeburg, South Carolina was established in 1896. Its original purpose was to train Afro-American youth in practical agriculture, mechanical arts, military tactics, and teaching. LOCATION: Urban campus in large town, 40 miles southeast of Columbia. DEGREES OFFERED: BA, BS, MA, MEd, PhD, EdD. ANNUAL EXPENSES: Tuition and fees $2,200. Room and board $2,736. Books and supplies $400. Other expenses $700. FALL TERM APPLICATIONS: $10 fee. $15 fee for out-of-state applicants. Closing date July 31. Applicants notified on a rolling basis. Must reply within 2 weeks. Audition required for music education applicants. Portfolio required for art education applicants. Deferred admission available. CONTACT: Benny R. Mayfield, Dean of Enrollment Management, South Carolina State College, Orangeburg, SC 29117-0001 (803) 536-7185.

SOUTHERN UNIVERSITY AGRICULTURE AND MECHANICAL (A&M) COLLEGE at Baton Rouge, Louisiana, was chartered in 1880 by the general assembly of the state of Louisiana. A few of its programs of distinction are the Afro-American executive exchange program, the congressional internship program, and the teacher corps program. A public affairs center on the main campus provides services to the surrounding community. LOCATION: Suburban campus in small city, 85-90 miles from New Orleans. DEGREES OFFERED: AA, AS, AAS, BA, BS, BArch, MA, MS, MEd, PhD, EdD, JD. ANNUAL EXPENSES: Tuition and fees $1,580; $1,522 additional for out-of-state students. Room and board $2,799. Books and supplies $500. Other expenses $500. FALL TERM APPLICATIONS: $5 fee. Closing date July 2. Applicants notified on a rolling basis. Early admission available. CONTACT: Henry J. Bellaire,

Director of Admissions and Recruitment, Southern
University A&M College, Southern Branch Post Office,
Baton Rouge, LA 70813 (504) 771-2430.

SOUTHWESTERN CHRISTIAN COLLEGE at Terrell,
Texas, was founded in 1949. Originally the school was called
the Southern Bible Institute. Its name was changed to
Southwestern Christian College in 1950 with the goal of
serving as a Christian college primarily for Afro-Americans of
the Church of Christ. LOCATION: Rural campus in large
town, 30 miles east of Dallas. DEGREES OFFERED: AA, BA,
BS. ANNUAL EXPENSES: Tuition and fees $3,640. Room and
board $2,307. Books and supplies $300. Other expenses $400.
FALL TERM APPLICATIONS: $10 fee. Closing date July 31.
Applicants notified on a rolling basis. Interview recom-
mended. Deferred and early admission available. CONTACT:
Gerald Lee, Director of Admissions, Southwestern Christian
College, P.O. Box 10, Terrell, TX 75160 (214) 524-3341.

SPELMAN COLLEGE at Atlanta, Georgia, was founded in
1881 and is the oldest and largest historically African-
American private undergraduate liberal arts college for
women. Spelman was founded as the first college for Afro-
American women in the United States. It grew out of a school
that was started in the basement of the Friendship Baptist
church. The school was called the Atlanta Baptist Female
Seminary. In 1883 it was moved to its present site, then
consisting of nine acres of land and five frame buildings that
had been used as drill grounds and barracks by Union troops
during the Civil War and that were later secured by the
American Baptist Home Mission Society. In 1884 the
school's name was changed to Spelman in honor of Mr. and
Mrs. Harvey Buel Spelman, the parents of Mrs. John D.

Rockefeller, because her husband had paid the newly founded school's debts. LOCATION: Urban campus in very large city, 2 miles from downtown. DEGREES OFFERED: BA, BS. ANNUAL EXPENSES: Tuition and fees $7,327. Room and board $5,000. Books and supplies $450. Other expenses $1,150. FALL TERM APPLICATIONS: $35 fee, may be waived for applicants with need. Closing date February 1. Applicants notified on or about March 15. Must reply by May 1. Interview recommended. Essay required. CONTACT: Aline A. Rivers, Executive Director of Enrollment Management, Spelman College, 350 Spelman Lane SW, Atlanta, GA 30314-4399 (404) 681-3643.

STILLMAN COLLEGE at Tuscaloosa, Alabama, was founded in 1876. Its purpose was to train African-American men for the ministry. It opened in a rented house and occupied two other sites before it was moved in 1898 to its present location, a former plantation, in 1898. LOCATION: Suburban campus in small city, 60 miles west of Birmingham. DEGREES OFFERED: BA, BS. ANNUAL EXPENSES: Tuition and fees $4,460. Room and board $2,754. Books and supplies $400. Other expenses $1,000. FALL TERM APPLICATIONS: $10 fee, may be waived for applicants with need. Closing date August 1. Priority given to applications received by May 1. Applicants notified on a rolling basis. Early admission available. CONTACT: Barbara K. Smith, Director of Admissions/Registrar, Stillman College, P.O. Box 1430, Tuscaloosa, AL 35403 (205) 349-4240 ext. 346/347.

TALLADEGA COLLEGE at Talladega, Alabama, was founded in 1867 and was the first college opened to Afro-Americans in the state of Alabama. LOCATION: Rural campus in small city, 60 miles east of Birmingham. DEGREES

OFFERED: BA. ANNUAL EXPENSES: Tuition and fees $4,453. Room and board $2,364. Books and supplies $600. Other expenses $500. FALL TERM APPLICATIONS: $10 fee. No closing date. Priority given to applications received by August 1. Applicants notified on a rolling basis. Must reply within 4 weeks. Audition required for music applicants. Early admission available. CONTACT: Mr. Monroe Thornton, Director of Admissions, Talladega College, 627 West Battle Street, Talladega, AL 35160 (205) 362-0206.

TEXAS COLLEGE at Tyler, Texas, was founded in 1894. LOCATION: Urban campus in small city, 90 miles east of Dallas, 90 miles west of Shreveport, Louisiana. DEGREES OFFERED: BA, BS. ANNUAL EXPENSES: Tuition and fees $3,605. Room and board $2,430. Books and supplies $400. Other expenses $925. FALL TERM APPLICATIONS: $5 fee, may be waived for applicants with need. Closing date August 15. Applicants notified on a rolling basis. Audition recommended for music applicants. Deferred and early admission available. CONTACT: Sandra L. Smith, Director of Admissions, Texas College, 2404 North Grand Avenue, Tyler, TX 75702-2404 (903) 593-8311.

TEXAS SOUTHERN UNIVERSITY at Houston, Texas, was founded in 1947 by the state legislature in response to legal pressures applied by Afro-Americans for equality in higher education. LOCATION: Urban campus in very large city, 2 miles from downtown Houston. DEGREES OFFERED: BA, BS, MA, MS, MBA, MEd, EdD. ANNUAL EXPENSES: Tuition and fees $1,030; $3,240 additional for out-of-state students. Room and board $3,320. Books and supplies $500. Other expenses $1,700. FALL TERM APPLICATIONS: $10 fee. $50 fee for international applicants. Closing date August 15. Priority given to applications received by July 31. Applicants notified on a rolling basis. CONTACT: Dr. Maude Guilford, Director of Admissions, Recruitment and Academic Advisement, Texas Southern University, 3100 Cleburne Street, Houston, TX 77004 (713) 527-7070.

TOUGALOO COLLEGE at Tougaloo, Mississippi, was founded in 1869 by the American Missionary Association of New York which purchased a plantation of five hundred acres for the training of newly freed slaves. LOCATION: Suburban campus in rural community near Jackson. DEGREES OFFERED: AA, BA. ANNUAL EXPENSES: Tuition and fees $5,090. Room and board $1,840. Books and supplies $500. Other expenses $500. FALL TERM APPLICATIONS: No fee. No closing date. Applicants notified on a rolling basis. Must reply within 2 weeks. Audition required for music applicants. Portfolio recommended for art applicants. Early admission available. CONTACT: Washington Cole IV, Director of Admissions and Recruiting, Tougaloo College, 500 West County Line Road, Tougaloo, MS 39174 (601) 977-7700 ext. 7770.

TUSKEGEE UNIVERSITY at Tuskegee, Alabama, was established in 1881 by an act of the general assembly of Alabama with Booker T. Washington as its founder and first principal. Washington stressed practical knowledge but at no time ignored the liberal arts, and the institute grew quickly from its original one room. In 1882 Washington contracted to buy a one-hundred-acre abandoned plantation which became the nucleus of Tuskegee's present campus near Montgomery. By 1970, the institute had grown from a single academic department to six schools and colleges, from thirty students to more than three thousand, and from a faculty of one to a faculty of two hundred fifty. LOCATION: Rural campus in large town, 40 miles from Montgomery. DEGREES OFFERED: BA, BS, BArch, MS, MEd. ANNUAL EXPENSES: Tuition and fees $6,535. Room and board $3,270. Books and supplies $550. Other expenses $1,050. FALL TERM APPLICATIONS: $15 fee, may be waived for applicants with need. Closing date July 15. Priority given to applications received by May 15. Applicants notified on a rolling basis beginning on or about March 1. Must reply by May 1 or within 2 weeks if notified thereafter. Interview recommended for veterinary medicine applicants. Essay required. Deferred and early admission available. CONTACT: Isaac Sanders, VP, Enrollment Management and Student Services, Tuskegee University, Tuskegee, AL 36088 (205) 727-8500.

UNIVERSITY OF THE DISTRICT OF COLUMBIA at Washington, DC, was created in 1977 from a merger of three local institutions. LOCATION: Urban campus in very large city. DEGREES OFFERED: AA, AS, BA, BS, MA, MS, MBA. ANNUAL EXPENSES: Tuition and fees $800; $2,880 additional for nondistrict students Books and supplies $600. Other expenses $1,400. FALL TERM APPLICATIONS: $10 fee. Closing date August 1. Priority given to applications received by July 1. Applicants notified on a rolling basis. Interview recommended for nursing applicants. Portfolio recommended for art applicants. Deferred admission available. CONTACT: Sandra Doldhin, Director of Admissions/Registrar, University of the District of Columbia, 4200 Connecticut Avenue NW, Washington, DC 20008 (202) 282-3200.

UNIVERSITY OF MARYLAND EASTERN SHORE at Princess Anne, Maryland, was founded in 1866 by Methodists. White students began to enroll beyond the "token" level during the 1960s, and by the early 1970s, they amounted to one fourth of the student body. LOCATION: Rural campus in rural community, 12 miles from Salisbury. DEGREES OFFERED: BA, BS, MA, MS, PhD. ANNUAL EXPENSES: Tuition and fees $2,486; $4,365 additional for out-of-state students. Room and board $3,580. Books and supplies $500. Other expenses $1,000. FALL TERM APPLICATIONS: $25 fee, may be waived for applicants with need. Closing date August 1. Priority given to applications received by April 1. Applicants notified on a rolling basis. Must reply within 2 weeks. Interview recommended for honors program and physical therapy applicants. Essay recommended. Deferred and early admission available. CONTACT: Rachell Peoples, Director of Admissions and Registrations, University of Maryland Eastern Shore, Princess Anne, MD 21853-1299 (410) 651-2200.

VIRGINIA STATE UNIVERSITY at Petersburg, Virginia, was founded in 1882 as a training institute for Afro-American citizens of Virginia. LOCATION: Suburban campus in large town, 25 miles from Richmond. DEGREES OFFERED: BA, BS, BFA, MA, MS, MEd. ANNUAL EXPENSES: Tuition and fees $2,913; $3,402 additional for out-of-state students. Room and board $4,127. Books and supplies $500. Other expenses $500. FALL TERM APPLICATIONS: $25 fee, may be waived for applicants with need. Closing date May 1. Priority given to applications received by March 31. Applicants notified on a rolling basis beginning on or about January 10. Must reply by May 1 or within 2 weeks if notified thereafter. Audition required for music applicants. Essay recommended. Deferred admission available. CONTACT: Karen R. Winston, Director of Admissions, Virginia State University, P.O. Box 18, Petersburg, VA 23803 (804) 524-5902.

VIRGINIA UNION UNIVERSITY at Richmond, Virginia, was founded in 1865. LOCATION: Urban campus in small city, 90 miles north of Norfolk, 100 miles south of Washington, DC. DEGREES OFFERED: BA, BS. ANNUAL EXPENSES: Tuition and fees $6,668. Room and board $3,384. Books and supplies $500. Other expenses $1,000. FALL TERM APPLICATIONS: $10 fee, may be waived for applicants with need. Closing date June 15. Priority given to applications received by April 1. Applicants notified on a rolling basis. Must reply within 2 weeks. Interview recommended for academically weak applicants. Audition required for music applicants. Essay recommended. Deferred admission available. CONTACT: Gil Powell, Director of Admissions, Virginia Union University, 1500 North Lombardy Street, Richmond, VA 23220 (804) 257-5856.

VOORHEES COLLEGE at Denmark, South Carolina, was founded in 1897 by Elizabeth Evelyn Wright, a graduate of Tuskegee Institute. LOCATION: Rural campus in small town, 50 miles from Columbia. DEGREES OFFERED: BS. ANNUAL EXPENSES: Tuition and fees $3,950. Room and board $2,522. Books and supplies $500. Other expenses $800. FALL TERM APPLICATIONS: $10 fee. No closing date. Applicants notified on a rolling basis, must reply within 2 weeks. Deferred admission available. CONTACT: Marian Thompson, Director of Admissions and Recruitment, Voorhees College, Voorhees Road, Denmark, SC 29042 (803) 793-3351.

WEST VIRGINIA STATE COLLEGE at Institute, West Virginia, was founded in 1891. Following the U.S. Supreme Court school desegregation decision of 1954, the college opened its doors to white students. LOCATION: Suburban campus in small town, 8 miles from Charleston. DEGREES OFFERED: AA, AS, AAS, BA, BS. ANNUAL EXPENSES: Tuition and fees $1,578; $2,110 additional for out-of-state students. Room and board $2,950. Books and supplies $440. Other expenses $940. FALL TERM APPLICATIONS: No fee. No closing date. Priority given to applications received by August 11. Applicants notified on a rolling basis. Interview recommended for nuclear medicine technology, academically weak, and bachelor of arts applicants. Deferred and early admission available. New students encouraged to apply for admission several months before a semester begins. CONTACT: Robin Green, Assistant Director of Admissions, West Virginia State College, P.O. Box 197, Institute, WV 25112-0335 (304) 766-3221.

WILBERFORCE UNIVERSITY at Wilberforce, Ohio, was founded in 1856. LOCATION: Rural campus in rural community, 18 miles east of Dayton. DEGREES OFFERED: BA, BS. ANNUAL EXPENSES: Tuition and fees $6,980. Room and board $3,564. Books and supplies $550. Other expenses $1,500. FALL TERM APPLICATIONS: $20 fee, may be waived for applicants with need. Closing date June 1. Applicants notified on a rolling basis. Must reply within 3 weeks. Interview recommended. Essay recommended. Deferred and early admission available. CONTACT: Karen Q. Preston, Assistant Director for Admissions, Wilberforce University, 1055 North Bickett Road, Wilberforce, OH 45384-1091 (513) 376-7321.

WILEY COLLEGE at Marshall, Texas, was founded in 1873. LOCATION: Urban campus in large town; 40 miles west of Shreveport, Louisiana. DEGREES OFFERED: AA, BA, BS. ANNUAL EXPENSES: Tuition and fees $3,946. Room and

board $2,544. Books and supplies $200. Other expenses $900.
FALL TERM APPLICATIONS: $10 fee. No closing date. Priority
given to applications received by September 15. Applicants
notified on a rolling basis. Must reply by May 1 or within 2
weeks if notified thereafter. Audition required for music
applicants. Deferred and early admission available.
CONTACT: Lee Marcus Roberts, Director of Admissions and
Recruitment, Wiley College, 711 Wiley Avenue, Marshall,
TX 75670 (903) 938-8341.

WINSTON-SALEM STATE UNIVERSITY at Winston-
Salem, North Carolina, was founded in 1892. LOCATION:
Urban campus in small city, 28 miles from Greensboro.
DEGREES OFFERED: BA, BS. ANNUAL EXPENSES: Tuition and
fees $1,060; $4,474 additional for out-of-state students. Room
and board $2,630. Books and supplies $600. Other expenses
$2,100. FALL TERM APPLICATIONS: $15 fee. No closing date.
Priority given to applications received by May 1. Applicants
notified on a rolling basis. Must reply within 3 weeks.
Interview recommended. Audition required for music appli-
cants. CONTACT: Van C. Wilson, Director of Admissions,
Winston-Salem State University, 601 Martin Luther King
Drive, Winston Salem, NC 27110. (919) 750-2070.

XAVIER UNIVERSITY OF LOUISIANA at New Orleans,
Louisiana, was founded in 1915. Xavier is the only predominantly black university in the United States that is operated
under Catholic auspices. The multiracial teaching faculty
consists of 104 laymen, 24 nuns, and 5 priests. Traditionally,
a high percentage of Xavier graduates have become teachers.
In 1965, 40 percent of the teachers, 75 percent of the
principals and 90 percent of the guidance counselors in the
Afro-American public schools in New Orleans were Xavier

alumni. LOCATION: Urban campus in very large city, one mile from downtown. DEGREES OFFERED: BA, BS, MA, MS, PharmD. ANNUAL EXPENSES: Tuition and fees $6,300. Room and board $3,400. Books and supplies $576. Other expenses $1,119. FALL TERM APPLICATIONS: $15 fee, may be waived for applicants with need. Closing date March 1. Applicants notified on or about April 1. Must reply by May 1. Interview recommended for academically weak applicants. Audition recommended for music applicants. Portfolio recommended for art applicants. Deferred admission available. CONTACT: Winston B. Brown, Dean of Admissions and Financial Aid, Xavier University of Louisiana, 7325 Palmetto Street, New Orleans, LA 70125 (504) 486-7411.

CHAPTER

3

Money for College

A college degree has traditionally been highly valued in the black community as the ticket to a middle class lifestyle. Unfortunately, recent federal cutbacks in financial aid has made it almost impossible for poor and middle-income black families to provide higher education for their children. Prospective students must turn to other sources for help.

There are many private sources of aid available, but you must be ingenious, persistent, and aggressive in your attempts to unearth all of them.

In this chapter, you will find information about some of the private sources of aid to students that are often overlooked or hard to find. As with federal financial aid, obtaining this money is a highly competitive process.

It is possible to gain an edge by having good grades, filing forms on a timely basis, and following up by phone on the status of your application.

Undergraduate
ACCOUNTING

TITLE: Minority Scholarship Program. ADMINISTERED BY: American Institute of Certified Public Accountants, 1211 Avenue of the Americas, New York, NY 10036 (212) 575-7641. AMOUNT: $1,500 per academic year. ELIGIBILITY: Black Americans, American Indians, Asians, and Hispanics who are U.S. citizens and studying accounting. DURATION: 1 year. DEADLINE: July 1 and December 1.

ARCHITECTURE

TITLE: AIA Minority/Disadvantaged Scholarship Program. ADMINISTERED BY: AIA Scholarship Program, The American Institute of Architects, 1735 New York Avenue NW, Washington, DC 20006. AMOUNT: Varies according to individual need. ELIGIBILITY: For high school graduates who are enrolled as freshmen in a professional program of architecture. DURATION: 1 year; renewable. DEADLINE: December 1.

BROADCASTING

TITLE: Thomas R. Dargan Minority Scholarship. ADMINISTERED BY: The Oregon Association of Broadcasters, P.O. Box 20037, Portland, Oregon 97220. AMOUNT: $3,500. ELIGIBILITY: Minority students enrolled in first, second, or third years of broadcast curriculum at colleges in Oregon and Washington. DURATION: 1 year. DEADLINE: April 30.

BUSINESS ADMINISTRATION

TITLE: Minority Foundation Scholarship. ADMINISTERED BY: Golden State Minority Foundation, 1999 West Adams Boulevard, Los Angeles, CA 90018 (213) 731-7771. AMOUNT: $1,500 - $2,000. ELIGIBILITY: Must be a U.S. citizen and minority upperclassman at a California college majoring in business administration. DURATION: 1 year. DEADLINE: Monthly.

DENTISTRY

TITLE: Juliette A. Southard Scholarship Trust Fund. ADMINISTERED BY: American Dental Assistants Association, 919 North Michigan Avenue, Suite 3400, Chicago, IL 60611. AMOUNT: $100-$200. ELIGIBILITY: Must be citizen of the United States and enrolled in a dental assisting teacher education program leading to a B.A. degree. DURATION: 1 year; renewable. DEADLINE: July 15.

EDUCATION

TITLE: Alabama Emergency Secondary Education Scholarships. ADMINISTERED BY: Alabama Commission on Higher Education, One Court Square Suite 221, Montgomery, AL 36197-0001. AMOUNT: $3,996; renewable. ELIGIBILITY: Must be a citizen of the United States and enrolled as a full time, upper division, undergraduate student in an approved school for teacher education. Must agree to teach in Alabama public schools for three years following completion of degree program. DURATION: 1 year; renewable. DEADLINE: June 1.

ELECTRICAL ENGINEERING

TITLE: Engineering Scholarships Program for Minorities and Women. ADMINISTERED BY: AT&T Bell Laboratories, Crawford's Corner Road, Room 1E-213, Holmdel, NJ 07733 (908) 949-4300. AMOUNT: Full tuition and fees. ELIGIBILITY: Minorities and women planning to enter the engineering profession; must maintain B average. DURATION: 1 year. DEADLINE: February 1.

FILMMAKING

TITLE: Black Filmmakers Grants Program. ADMINISTERED BY: Black Filmmakers Association, 3617 Mont Clair Street, Los Angeles, CA 90018 (213) 737-3292. AMOUNT: $1,500. ELIGIBILITY: Applications must be made in the name of individual(s) who have primary creative responsibility for the production. Applicant(s) must be U.S. citizen and project must be made in the United States. Only one project per grant cycle may be submitted. The project must be in 16mm or 3/4 inch video. DEADLINE: January 15.

HEALTH

TITLE: American Foundation for Aging Research Fellowship. ADMINISTERED BY: American Foundation for Aging Research, North Carolina State University, Biochemistry Department, 128 Polk Hall, Box 7622, Raleigh, NC 27695-7622. AMOUNT: $500-$1,000. ELIGIBILITY: Must be undergraduate actively involved or be planning active involvement in a specific biomedical research project in the field of aging. DURATION: 1 year. DEADLINE: None.

TITLE: American Heart Association Student Research Program. ADMINISTERED BY: Chairman, Student Research Sub-Committee, American Heart Association, California

Affiliate, 805 Burlway Road, Burlingame, CA 94010
(415) 342-5522. AMOUNT: $1,500. ELIGIBILITY: Mus
enrolled in a college or university at the time of application.
Must be attending an institution in California or be a resident
of California. Preference given to students with superior
academic standing who will have junior or senior status
for the first time in the fall. Must have primary interest in
research and a familiarity with chemical, biochemical and/or
physiological principles.

JOURNALISM

TITLE: NABJ Scholarship Program. ADMINISTERED BY:
National Association of Black Journalists, Box 17212,
Washington, DC 20041 (703) 648-1270. AMOUNT: $2,500.
ELIGIBILITY: Open to black undergraduates or graduate
students who are accepted to/enrolled in an accredited
journalism program majoring in print, photo, radio,
television, or planning a career in one of those areas.
DEADLINE: March 31.

MATHEMATICS

TITLE: AT&T Dual Degree Scholarship Program.
ADMINISTERED BY: AT&T Bell Laboratories, Crawfords
Corner Road, Room 1B-208, Holmdel, NJ 07733-1988
(201) 949-5424. AMOUNT: The program provides full
tuition, books, fees, room and board, a challenging summer
job each year at AT&T, and an appropriate mentor.
ELIGIBILITY: Through a Dual Degree scholars earn a B.A. in
mathematics or physics from Spelman, Morehouse, Clark, or
Morris Brown Colleges in three years and then go on to an
M.S. degree in engineering or computer science. DEADLINE:
December of each year.

NURSING

TITLE: Dr. Lauranne Sams Scholarship and Ambi Scholarship. ADMINISTERED BY: National Black Nurses Association Inc, P.O. Box 18358, Boston, MA 02118 (617) 266-9703. AMOUNT: $1,000 and $4,000. ELIGIBILITY: Students recently enrolled in a nursing program (A.D. Diploma; BSN; LPN/LVN) in good scholastic standing. Association members given preference. DURATION: 1 year; renewable. DEADLINE: April 15.

PHYSICS

TITLE: AT&T Dual Degree Scholarship Program. ADMINISTERED BY: AT&T Bell Laboratories, Crawfords Corner Road, Room lB-208, Holmdel, NJ 07733-1988 (201) 949-5424. AMOUNT: The program provides full tuition, books, fees, room and board, a challenging summer job each year at AT&T, and an appropriate mentor. ELIGIBILITY: Talented women and minorities who wish to enter the field of engineering. Through a Dual Degree program, scholars earn a B.A. in mathematics or physics from Spelman, Morehouse, Clark, or Morris Brown Colleges in three years and then go on to an M.S. degree in engineering or computer science. DEADLINE: December of each year.

SCIENCE

TITLE: Minority Participation Program Scholarships. ADMINISTERED BY: American Geological Institute, 4220 King Street, Alexandria, VA 22302 (703) 379-2480. AMOUNT: $500-$1,500. ELIGIBILITY: Open to American Blacks, Native Americans, Hispanic Americans. Must be U.S. citizen. DURATION: 1 year; renewable. DEADLINE: February 1.

THEOLOGY

TITLE: Benjamin E. Mays Fellowships. ADMINISTERED BY: Fund for Theological Education, 475 Riverside Drive #832, New York, NY 10115 (212) 870-2058. AMOUNT: Varies. ELIGIBILITY: Fellowships for outstanding black North American students who are interested in becoming Protestant ministers. Must be U.S. or Canadian citizen. DEADLINE: November 20.

VARIOUS AREAS

TITLE: AAL All-College Scholarship Program. ADMINISTERED BY: Aid Association for Lutherans, 4321 North Ballard Road, Appleton, WI 54919 (414) 734-5721. AMOUNT: $500-$2,000. ELIGIBILITY: Must be of good character and have grades which meet the entrance standards at the Lutheran college or university of your choice. DURATION: 1 year; renewable. DEADLINE: November 30.

TITLE: Alpha Kappa Alpha Scholarships. ADMINISTERED BY: Alpha Kappa Alpha Sorority, 5656 South Stony Island Avenue, Chicago, IL 60637 (312) 684-1282. AMOUNT: Stipends are usually $1,000. ELIGIBILITY: Most of the 700 local chapters award scholarships to deserving high school students in their communities.

TITLE: Catholic Negro Scholarship Fund. ADMINISTERED BY: Catholic Scholarships for Negroes, Inc., P.O Box 1730, Springfield, MA 01101-1730. AMOUNT: Between $100 and $500 per year. ELIGIBILITY: For black students about to enter or wishing to continue college. DURATION: 1 year; renewable.

TITLE: Educational Fund Scholarship. ADMINISTERED BY: Racine Environment Committee, 310 Fifth Street, Room 101, Racine, WI 53403 (414) 631-5600. AMOUNT: $1,200. ELIGIBILITY: Minority students who are residents of Racine Wisconsin. DURATION: 1 year. DEADLINE: June 30 and October 31.

TITLE: Henry Sachs Scholarship Fund. ADMINISTERED BY: Henry Sachs Foundation (Scholarship Program), 101 North Cascade Avenue, Suite 430, Colorado Springs, CO 80903 (303) 633-2353. AMOUNT: $2,250. ELIGIBILITY: Open to black residents of Colorado who are high school graduates. Awards are for undergraduate or graduate study at any accredited college or university. DURATION: 1 year; renewable if student maintains a "C" or better average.

TITLE: Need Scholarship Program. ADMINISTERED BY: Negro Educational Emergency Drive, 643 Liberty Avenue, 17th Floor, Pittsburgh, PA 15222 (412) 566-2760. AMOUNT: $100-$1,000. ELIGIBILITY: Open to black residents with a high school diploma or GED who reside in Allegheny, Armstrong, Beaver, Butler, Washington, or Westmoreland counties. DEADLINE: May 13.

TITLE: Scholarship Program. ADMINISTERED BY: United Negro College Fund, 500 East 62nd Street, New York, NY 10021 (212) 644-9600. AMOUNT: $1,200 maximum per year. ELIGIBILITY: Scholarships available to all students who enroll in one of the 43 United Negro College Fund member institutions. DURATION: Previous recipients are granted a renewal if they are able to maintain a "B" average. DEADLINE: August.

TITLE: Virginia State Assistance To Children of Veterans. ADMINISTERED BY: Virginia Department of Veterans' Affairs, P.O. Box 809, Roanoke, VA 24004. AMOUNT: Qualified recipients are allowed to attend state supported colleges tuition free. ELIGIBILITY: Must be the son or daughter of a veteran who was a citizen of Virginia at the time of entering war service. Open only to children of veterans deceased or totally and permanently disabled from service connected causes. Must be at least 16 but not more than 25 years of age. DURATION: Four years. DEADLINE: None.

Graduate School
AFRO-AMERICAN STUDIES

TITLE: Afro-American and African Studies Pre-Doctoral Fellowship. ADMINISTERED BY: Carter G. Woodson Institute for Afro-American and African Studies, University of Virginia, 1512 Jefferson Park Avenue, Charlottesville, VA 22903 (804) 924-3109, Attn: Associate Director for Research. AMOUNT: $12,500 per year. ELIGIBILITY: Applicants must have completed all requirements for the Ph.D. in Afro-American or African studies except for the dissertation prior to August of the fellowship year. Affiliates of the University of Virginia may not apply. Fellows must be in residence at the University of Virginia for the duration of the award period. They are expected to contribute to the intellectual life of the university. DEADLINE: December of each year.

TITLE: Center for Black Studies Fellowships. ADMINISTERED BY: Center for Black Studies, University of California at Santa Barbara, South Hall 4603, Santa Barbara, CA 93106-3140 (805) 961-8000. AMOUNT: The stipend is $16,000. ELIGIBILITY: Candidates must be enrolled in a doctoral program and working on a dissertation in black studies at an accredited university. DURATION: 9 months. DEADLINE: February of each year.

BUSINESS ADMINISTRATION

TITLE: Fellowships For Minorities. ADMINISTERED BY: Consortium for Graduate Study In Management, Box 1132, One Brookings Dr, St. Louis, MO 63163 (314) 889-6353. AMOUNT: Full tuition and $5,000 stipend over 2 years. ELIGIBILITY: Open to Blacks, Native Americans, and Hispanic Americans who are U.S. citizens and have received BA degree from accredited institution. DEADLINE: March 1.

EDUCATION

TITLE: Martin Luther King Jr. Memorial Scholarship Fund. ADMINISTERED BY: California Teachers Association, P.O. Box 921, 1705 Murchison Drive, Burlingame, CA 94010 (415) 697-1400. AMOUNT: $250-$2,000. ELIGIBILITY: Open to any active member of CTA or student CTA (SCTA) who is a California resident, U.S. citizen and either Black, Hispanic, American Indian, Alaska native, or Pacific Islander. DEADLINE: March 15.

ENGINEERING

TITLE: National Consortium Fellowship. ADMINISTERED BY: National Consortium for Graduate Degrees for Minorities, Inc., P.O. Box 537, Notre Dame, IN 46556 (219) 239-7183. AMOUNT: Full tuition and fees plus $5,000 stipend. Award also includes paid summer research work experience. ELIGIBILITY: Fellowships for Native Americans, Black Americans, Mexican Americans and Puerto Ricans who are U.S. citizens. DEADLINE: December 1.

GENEALOGY

TITLE: Creole Scholarship Fund. ADMINISTERED BY: Creole Ethnic Association, Inc., P.O. Box 2666, Church Street

Station, New York, NY 10008. AMOUNT: $1,000.
ELIGIBILITY: To individuals of mixed racial ancestry who
are U.S. citizens and at least 1/32 black. Application must
include a genealogy chart of at least 5 generations.
DEADLINE: June 30.

GEOSCIENCES

TITLE: AGI Minority Graduate Scholarships.
ADMINISTERED BY: American Geological Institute, 4220
King Street, Alexandria, VA 22302-1507 (703) 379-2480.
AMOUNT: Up to $4,000 per year. ELIGIBILITY: Selection
is based on academic excellence and likelihood of future
success in the geosciences profession. DEADLINE: Varies.

JOURNALISM

TITLE: NABJ Scholarship Program. ADMINISTERED BY:
National Association of Black Journalists, Box 17212,
Washington, DC 20041 (703) 648-1270. AMOUNT: $2,500.
ELIGIBILITY: Open to Black undergraduates or graduate
students who are accepted to/enrolled in an accredited journalism program majoring in print, photo, radio, television, or
planning a career in one of those areas. DEADLINE: March 31.

LAW

TITLE: Earl Warren Scholarship Program. ADMINISTERED
BY: Earl Warren Legal Training Program, 99 Hudson Street,
16th Floor, New York, NY 10013 (212) 219-1900. AMOUNT:
Varies. ELIGIBILITY: For entering black law students under
35 years of age. U.S. citizenship required and must submit
proof of acceptance to an accredited law school. Emphasis
on applicants who wish to enter law schools in the South.
DEADLINE: March 15.

LIBRARY SCIENCE

TITLE: Charlemae Hill Rollins Scholarship. ADMINISTERED BY: National Black Caucus of Librarians, Chicago Chapter, c/o Emma Kemp, 8101 South Evans Street, Chicago, IL 60619. AMOUNT: The stipend is $300. ELIGIBILITY: Black college graduates who live in the Chicago area, have an excellent academic record, and have completed no more than 12 semester credits toward graduate degree in library science. DURATION: 1 year; nonrenewable. DEADLINE: February of each year.

MEDICINE

TITLE: NMP Special Award and Fellowship Progams. ADMINISTERED BY: National Medical Fellowships, 254 West 31st Street, New York, NY 10001 (212) 714-0933. AMOUNT: Up to $5,000. ELIGIBILITY: Open to black and Puerto Rican students accepted to or enrolled in U.S. medical schools. DEADLINES: April 30, August 30.

NURSING

TITLE: Estelle M. Osborne Scholarship Fund. ADMINISTERED BY: Nurses Educational Funds Inc., 555 West 57th Street, New York, NY 10019 (212) 582-8820. AMOUNT: $1,000-$5,000. ELIGIBILITY: Open to black RNs who are U.S. citizens and enrolled in an accredited master's program in nursing. DEADLINE: March 1.

POLITICAL SCIENCE

TITLE: APSA Graduate Fellowships for Black American Students. ADMINISTERED BY: American Political Science Association, 1527 New Hampshire Avenue NW, Washington,

DC 20036 (202) 483-2512. AMOUNT: $6,000. ELIGIBILITY: Preference given to those students just starting their masters or doctorate program. Must be U.S. citizen. DEADLINE: December 1.

SCIENCE

TITLE: Minority Participation Program Scholarships. ADMINISTERED BY: American Geological Institute, 4220 King Street, Alexandria, VA 22302, (703) 379-2480. AMOUNT: $500-$1,500. ELIGIBILITY: For undergraduate or graduate study in science. DEADLINE: February 1.

URBAN PLANNING

TITLE: Minority Fellowship Program. ADMINISTERED BY: American Planning Association, 1776 Massachusetts Avenue NW, Washington, DC 20036 (202) 872-0611. AMOUNT: $1,000. ELIGIBILITY: Open to U.S./Canadian citizens who are Black, Mexican-American, North American Indian or Puerto Rican and demonstrate financial need. DEADLINE: May 15.

VARIOUS AREAS

TITLE: AT&T Cooperative Research Fellowship Program. ADMINISTERED BY: AT&T Bell Laboratories, Attn: CRFP Program Administrator, 101 Crawfords Corner Road, P.O. Box 3030, Holmdel, NJ 07733-3030 (908) 949-2943. AMOUNT: This program covers tuition and fees, a textbook allowance, a $13,200 annual stipend and conference travel. ELIGIBILITY: For outstanding African-Americans, Hispanic Americans and Native Americans who are college seniors and interested in pursuing a Ph.D. degree in chemistry, chemical engineering, electrical engineering, information science, materials science, mathematics, mechanical engineering, physics, or statistics. DURATION: 1 academic year plus a summer internship; may be renewed. DEADLINE: January of each year.

TITLE: McKnight Black Doctoral Fellowship Program. ADMINISTERED BY: Florida Endowment Fund for Higher Education, 201 E. Kennedy Blvd, Suite 1525, Tampa, FL 33602 (813) 221-2772. AMOUNT: $11,000 stipend and $5,000 tuition and fees (per year). ELIGIBILITY: Open to all black Americans with at least a BA degree from an accredited institution who wish to pursue a doctoral degree. Program recruits nationwide, however fellows must enroll in a Florida institution. DURATION: Renewable for three years. DEADLINE: January 15.

TITLE: Henry Sachs Scholarship Program. ADMINISTERED BY: Henry Sachs Foundation, 101 North Cascade Avenue, Suite 430, Colorado Springs, CO 80903 (303) 633-2353. AMOUNT: $2,250. ELIGIBILITY: Open to black residents of Colorado who are high school graduates. DURATION: Renewable if student maintains a "C" or better average. Grants are for up to 4 years in duration. DEADLINE: March 1.

TITLE: Agnes Jones Jackson Scholarship. ADMINISTERED BY: National Association for the Advancement of Colored People, Attention: Director of Education, 4805 Mt. Hope Drive, Baltimore, MD 21215 (410) 358-8900. AMOUNT: The stipend is $1,500 for undergraduate students and $2,500 for graduate students. ELIGIBILITY: Open to members of the NAACP who are attending college on a full time basis. Graduating high school students must possess a grade point average of 2.5, undergraduate students 2.0, and graduate students 3.0. All applicants must be able to demonstrate financial need, be under the age of 25, and be U.S. citizens. DURATION: l year; recipients may apply for renewal. DEADLINE: April of each year.

TITLE: Virginia State Assistance To Children of Veterans. ADMINISTERED BY: Virginia Department of Veterans' Affairs, P.O. Box 809, Roanoke, VA 24004. AMOUNT: Qualified recipients are allowed to attend state supported universities, tuition free. ELIGIBILITY: Must be the son or daughter of a veteran who was a citizen of Virginia at the time of entering war service. Open only to children of veterans deceased or totally and permanently disabled from service connected causes. Must be at least 16 but not more than 25 years of age. DURATION: Three years. DEADLINE: None.

TITLE: W.E.B. Du Bois Fellowship. ADMINISTERED BY: West Virginia University, Office of Admissions & Records, Box 6009, Morgantown, WV 26506 (304) 293-2124. AMOUNT: $5,200. ELIGIBILITY: Applicants must have bachelors degree from an accredited college or university and be admitted to a graduate or professional program at West Virginia University. DEADLINE: March of each year.

CHAPTER

Cultural Organizations

There are literally hundreds of community and cultural organizations across the country that are seeking to improve one or more aspects of African-American life. Typical causes include consciousness raising, political action, helping black colleges to survive, working for better housing, education, and job training. Whatever your interests are, there is a place for you. However, before volunteering, contact representatives from the list of organizations below and ask for detailed information to make sure that the philosophy, history, and services that the organization provides matches your own beliefs. This may take some time but don't postpone getting involved. There are many issues that need to be addressed, and the cultural organizations need all the skilled and hard-working volunteers they can find.

AFRICAN-AMERICAN DANCE COMPANY
394 Fifth Avenue, San Francisco, CA 94118
(415) 386-2832
Founded: 1980   Members: 100

This enterprise works to uphold the African-American culture in the world of dance.

AFRICAN-AMERICAN HISTORICAL & CULTURAL SOCIETY
Fort Mason Center, Building C, Room 165
San Francisco, CA 94123
(415) 441-0640

Upholds the traditions and culture of African and African-American people. Collects and distributes material. Maintains museum, gallery, and archives. Although activities are commonly held in the San Francisco Bay area, members are nationwide.

AFRICAN HERITAGE CENTER FOR AFRICAN DANCE AND MUSIC
4018 Minnesota Avenue NE, Washington, DC 20019
(202) 399-5252
Founded: 1973   Members: 20

Serves as a multicultural center for instruction and training in established West African dance, music, and dramatic ritualistic forms. This group is also for cross-cultural workshops between ethnic groups. Accepts traveling artists from abroad for workshops and exchange. Offers instruction in modern and jazz dance.

AFRICAN HERITAGE FEDERATION
OF THE AMERICAS

Kwanzaa

P.O. Box 3833, Pittsburgh, PA 15230
(412) 361-8425
Founded: 1983   Members: 36

People of African ancestry striving to encourage knowledge
and comprehension of African heritage. Conducts educational
programs; sponsors charitable programs; maintains speakers'
bureau; compiles statistics.

AFRICAN NATIONAL PEOPLE'S EMPIRE
RE-ESTABLISHED

c/o William Bert Johnson
18900 Schoolcraft, Detroit, MI 48223
Founded: 1951   Members: 351,642

Promotes the health, education, and welfare of African
people. Conducts specialized education programs.

AFRO-AMERICAN CULTURAL FOUNDATION

c/o Westchester Community College
75 Grasslands Rd., Valhalla, NY 10595
Founded: 1969   Members: 500

Purposes are to improve the self esteem of African-
Americans; to improve the attitude of white people toward
African-Americans and their talents; to boost the level
of awareness of the aptitudes and problems of African-
Americans; to help create a new self image. Sponsors lectures
and seminars. Conducts an annual workshop known as the
Institute of Racism.

ALABAMA BLACK LEGISLATIVE CAUCUS
P.O. Box 11385, Birmingham, AL 35202
(205) 322-3344

This is a political action organization which wants more involvement of blacks in the political process and to make government more responsive to black needs.

ASSOCIATION FOR THE PRESERVATION AND PRESENTATION OF THE ARTS
2011 Benning Road NE, Washington, DC 20002
(202) 529-3244
Founded 1964   Members: 500

Serves as a vehicle for the promotion of blacks in the arts. Seeks to increase public awareness and appreciation of the arts and its representation of African-American culture. Works on the development of musical and dance productions. Produces children's shows; sponsors lectures.

BLACK CITIZENS FOR A FAIR MEDIA
156-20 Riverside Drive No. 13L, New York, NY 10032
(212) 568-3168
Founded: 1971   Members: 250

Community organization concerned with hiring procedures in the television industry, images of black people on television, and how these images affect viewers.

BLACK FILMMAKERS HALL OF FAME
405 14th Street Suite 515, Oakland, CA 94612
(415) 465-0804
Founded: 1973 Members: 500

Seeks to study, teach, and preserve the contributions of black filmmakers to American cinema. Fosters cultural awareness through educational, research, and public service programs in the film arts. Holds film-lecture series, Black Filmworks Festival and International Film Competition.

BLACK MEN, INC.

105 East 22nd Street, New York, NY 10036
(212) 777-7070

This organization works to improve the life of blacks and other minorities in this country. Its efforts include better housing, education, employment, and gaining power in the professions and government.

BLACK PAC

P.O. Drawer 6865, McLean, VA 22106
(703) 442-7510
Founded: 1984   Members: 200

Represents political concerns of working class and middle class African-Americans. Does not lobby but aids in the election of favorable candidates to Congress.

BLACK RESOURCES INFORMATION COORDINATING SERVICES

614 Howard Avenue, Tallahassee, FL 32304
(904) 576-7522
Founded: 1972   Members: 670

Designed to bring together various sources of information and research by and about minority groups in America. Turns them into an orderly information system by using bibliographic control, storage, retrieval, transfer, and dissemination.

BLACK WOMEN OF COLOR
P.O. Box 2624, Binghamton, NY 13901
(607) 722-6519

This organization was formed to help black women face and resolve some of the problems they encounter and help them enter into the mainstream of life in America. It seeks to have women help each other in time of need.

BLACK WOMEN ORGANIZED FOR EDUCATIONAL DEVELOPMENT
518 17th Street Suite 202, Oakland, CA 94612
(510) 763-9501
Founded 1984   Members: 500

Supports self-sufficiency in and encourages empowerment of low-income and socially disadvantaged women by initiating and maintaining programs that improve their social and economic well being.

BUFFALO INNER CITY BALLET COMPANY
25 High Street, Buffalo, NY 14203
(716) 881-5131

This group provides a method for the area's inner city residents to express themselves and their concerns through the mode of dance.

CULTURAL SURVIVAL INC.
53A Church Street, Cambridge, MA 02138
(617) 495-2562
Founded 1972   Members: 18,000

Helps indigenous people survive, both physically and culturally, the rapid innovations brought on by contact with an expanding industrial society.

EAST BALTIMORE COMMUNITY CORP.

1700 North Gay Street, Baltimore, MD 21213
(301) 342-3481

This group has initiated a number of projects to aid
minorities in the East Baltimore area including job training,
counseling, youth services, health and drug abuse programs.

FOUNDATION FOR RESEARCH IN THE AFRO-AMERICAN CREATIVE ARTS

P.O. Drawer I, Cambria Heights, NY 11411
Founded: 1971   Members: 1,000

Promotes research into the Afro-American creative arts
including music, theater, and dance. Maintains small library
on black music and history, including fifteen taped oral
histories of black musicians.

FRIENDS OF THE HAITIANS

1023 Clouet Street, New Orleans, LA 70117
(504) 947-2717

This organization seeks to aid Haitian refugees by providing
shelter and food.

INSTITUTE FOR THE ADVANCED STUDY OF BLACK FAMILY LIFE AND CULTURE

175 Filbert Street–Suite 202, Oakland, CA 94607
(415) 836-3245

Seeks to bring together African-American families and to
strengthen the black community. Promotes the reclamation
of historic African-American culture. Develops training
curricula for teen parents. Maintains speakers' bureau.

INTERNATIONAL BLACK WOMEN'S CONGRESS
1081 Bergen Street, Newark, NJ 07112
(201) 926-0570
Founded: 1983   Members: 5,800

Objective is to unite members through annual networking tours to Africa, organize support groups, and aid women in starting their own businesses.

JACK AND JILL OF AMERICA
1065 Ralph David Abernathy Blvd. SW, Atlanta, GA 30310
(404) 753-8471
Founded: 1938   Members: 37,000

Objectives are to develop a medium of contact among African-American children to activate growth and development and to give them a productive cultural, civic, recreational, and social agenda.

NATIONAL BLACK LEADERSHIP ROUNDTABLE
2135 Rayburn House Bldg., Washington, DC 20515
Founded: 1983   Members: 300

Goals are to provide an arena for leaders of black associations to discuss and trade ideas on matters important to black Americans.

NATIONAL BLACK ON BLACK LOVE CAMPAIGN
401 N. Michigan Avenue 24th Floor, Chicago, IL 60611
(312) 644-6610
Founded: 1983   Members: 20,000

Seeks to encourage love and respect in all communities where black people are excessively touched by crime.

NATIONAL BLACK SURVIVAL FUND

P.O. Box 3005, Lafayette, LA 70502
(318) 232-7672
Founded: 1982   Members: 5,000

Theorizes that the economic, cultural, and physical survival
of the nation's black community is imperiled due to the
recession, discrimination, and federal cutbacks in social
assistance programs. Seeks to maintain and expand support
for programs that can deflect the economic and human
tragedy which could result if opportunities offered to blacks
are thwarted.

NATIONAL BLACK WOMEN'S CONSCIOUSNESS RAISING ASSOCIATION

1906 N. Charles Street, Baltimore, MD 21218
(301) 727-8900
Founded: 1975   Members: 750

Acts as a support group. Provides educational and
informational workshops and seminars on subjects
of concern to black women.

NATIONAL CAUCUS AND CENTER ON BLACK AGED

1424 K Street NW Suite 500, Washington, DC 20005
(202) 637-8400
Founded: 1970   Members: 300

Seeks to improve living conditions for low-income elderly
Americans, particularly blacks. Champions changes in federal
and state laws to improve the economic, health, and social
status of low-income senior citizens. Promotes community
understanding of problems and issues affecting the low-
income aging population.

NATIONAL HOOK-UP OF BLACK WOMEN
c/o Wynetta Frazier
5117 S. University Avenue, Chicago, IL 60615
Founded: 1975   Members: 500

Goal is to provide a communications network in support
of black women who serve in organizational leadership
positions.

NATIONAL ORGANIZATION OF BLACK COLLEGE ALUMNI
4 Washington Square Village No. 15E, New York, NY 10012
(212) 986-7726
Founded: 1982   Members: 5,000

For graduates, friends, and supporters of the historically
black colleges. Works to guarantee the survival of black
colleges by dealing with their concerns and needs and
providing resources to satisfy these requirements.

NEW AFRIKAN PEOPLE'S ORGANIZATION
13206 Dexter, Detroit, MI 48238
Founded: 1984   Members: 125

Favors an independent black nation in the American Deep
South. Wants to form a national awareness favorable to the
group's goals. Maintains Malcolm X Community Centers to
educate blacks about the struggle for black independence.
Collects food and clothing for the needy.

TRANSAFRICA
545 8th Street Suite 200, Washington, DC 20003
(202) 547-2550
Founded: 1977   Members: 8,000

Involved with the political and human rights of people in Africa and the Caribbean and those of African descent around the world. Attempts to influence U.S. foreign policy in these areas by informing the public of violations of social, political, and civil rights.

UNIVERSAL NEGRO IMPROVEMENT ASSOCIATION AND AFRICAN COMMUNITIES LEAGUE OF THE WORLD

5131 S. Wabash Avenue, Chicago, IL 60615
Founded: 1914 Members: 30,000

Individuals of African descent who are supporters of the group's founder Marcus Garvey (1887-1940). Thinks that the development of a United States of Africa will alleviate racial tension throughout the world. Promotes pride in and love for African heritage and culture while maintaining respect and love for different races.

WOMEN'S AFRICA COMMITTEE OF THE AFRICAN-AMERICAN INSTITUTE

833 United Nations Plaza, New York, NY 10017
(212) 949-5666
Founded: 1959

Volunteer organization of African and American women. Members seek to become better acquainted through social, educational, and cultural activities.

Places To Go
Things To Do

Whether you are planning an extended trip or just a weekend getaway, you will find all the current detailed information that you need in order to plan a fun and stimulating cultural vacation. States are arranged alphabetically followed by descriptions of notable attractions most likely to interest African-Americans. There is a balance of recreational, historical, and educational activities all centered around the acknowledgment and appreciation of African-American contributions to American life.

Alabama

ALABAMA SPORTS HALL OF FAME

Birmingham-Jefferson Civic Center
2150 Civic Center Boulevard, Birmingham, AL 35203
(205) 323-6665
Wed-Sat and holidays 10-5. Tues & Sun 1-5.
Adults $1.50. Students and seniors 75 cents. Under 6 Free.

Honors the role Joe Louis, Jesse Owens, Hank Aaron, Willie
Mays, and John Stallworth played in Alabama sports history.

BIRMINGHAM CIVIL RIGHTS INSTITUTE

520 Sixteenth Street North, Birmingham, AL 35204
(205) 328-9696

Houses multimedia exhibits, informational archives,
community meeting rooms, galleries. The institute also
hosts several cultural programs that tell of the events that
took place in Birmingham nearly thirty years ago.

W. C. HANDY HOME AND MUSEUM

620 West College Street, Florence, AL
Tues-Sat 9 to noon and 1-4. Closed January 1, July 4, and
December 23-25. Adults $1. Children under 18 free.

The restored log cabin home of the composer who has been
called the "father of the blues." Attached to the home is a
museum tracing Handy's career.

ST. PAUL AME ZION CHURCH

Cherokee Street, Florence, AL

Founded in 1806, both W. C. Handy's father and grandfather
had been pastors of the church and the Handy stained-glass
window given to the church can still be seen.

California

FOWLER MUSEUM OF CULTURAL HISTORY
UCLA
405 Hilgard Avenue, Los Angeles, CA 90024-1431
(310) 825-4361

Has one of the nation's leading collections of African art, founded in 1787. This building was a station of the underground railroad.

LOS ANGELES COUNTY MUSEUM OF ART
5905 Wilshire Boulevard, Los Angeles, CA 90036
(213) 857-6000
Tues-Fri 10-5. Weekends 10-6.
Adults $3. Seniors and students $1.50. Ages 5-12 75 cents.
Free on second Tuesday of each month.

Paintings by Black American artists and collectors of African sculpture.

CALIFORNIA AFRO-AMERICAN MUSEUM
600 State Drive, Exposition Park, Los Angeles, CA 90037
(213) 744-7432
Daily 10-5. Free.

Designed by a black architect, this museum has a theater, research library and galleries which are all devoted to the study of African-American life.

MUSEUM OF AFRICAN-AMERICAN ART
4005 Crenshaw Boulevard, Los Angeles, CA 90008-2534
(213) 294-7071
Thurs 12-8. Fri-Sat 11-6. Sun 12-5.
Free.

The museum houses traditional works such as the soapstones of the Shona people and contemporary pieces by black artists.

EBONY MUSEUM OF ART
1034 14th Street, Oakland, CA 94607
(510) 763-0141
Tues-Sat 11-6 and by appointment.
Adults $5. Children $2.

Paintings by African-Americans and exhibits on black history.

SAN FRANCISCO AFRICAN-AMERICAN HISTORICAL AND CULTURAL SOCIETY
Fort Mason Center, Building C Room 165, Buchanan Street and Marina Boulevard, San Francisco, CA 94123
(415) 441-0640
Wed-Sun 12-5. Closed holidays.
Adults $1. Children 50 cents.

African-Haitian artifacts, historical collections, guided tours, films, gallery talks, concerts.

Colorado

DENVER ART MUSEUM
100 W. 14th Avenue, Denver, CO 80204
(303) 640-2793
Tues-Sat 10-5. Sun 12-5. Closed holidays.
Adults $3. Over 65 and students $1.50. Under 6 free.

African Art and sculpture.

COLORADO HISTORY MUSEUM
13th and Broadway, Denver, CO 80203
(303) 866-3682
Mon-Sat 10-4:30. Sun 12-4:30. Closed Thanksgiving
and Dec. 25. Adults $2.50. Seniors and ages 6-16 $1.

Exhibit on African-American history including the role
of blacks in fur trade, pioneer days, and the gold rush.

AMERICAN WEST MUSEUM AND HERITAGE CENTER
3091 California Street, Denver, CO 86205
(303) 292-2566
Wed-Fri 10-2. Sat 12-5. Sun 2-5.
Adults $2. Seniors $1.50. Children 50 cents.

Showcases blacks in the west during the nineteenth century
and memorabilia of blacks who contributed to early Denver
history.

Connecticut

HARRIET BEECHER STOWE HOUSE
73 Forest Street, Hartford, CT 06105
(203) 525-9317
Tues-Sat 9:30-4. Sun noon-4.
Adults $6.50. Ages 6-12 $2.75.

Restored house of *Uncle Tom's Cabin* author contains many
furnishings and mementos of the writer.

CONNECTICUT AFRO-AMERICAN HISTORICAL SOCIETY
444 Orchard Street, New Haven, CT
(203) 776-4907
Mon 11:30-1:30 and by appointment.
Free.

A research center and museum with exhibits on the role of Afro-Americans in building Connecticut and America.

Delaware

JOHN DICKINSON PLANTATION
6 miles south of Dover on U.S. 113
then 1/2 mile east on Kitts-Hummock Road
Tues-Sat 10-4:30. Sun 1:30-4:30. Closed holidays.
Free.

Boyhood home of the colonial patriot has been restored to its early eighteenth century appearance, and visitors can see how slaves and freed blacks lived and worked in the house and fields.

OLD TOWN HALL MUSEUM
512 Market Street Mall, Wilmington, DE
Tues-Fri noon-4. Sat 10-4. Closed major holidays.
Donations.

Exhibits portray the role of the city's black community from the abolition movement to the 1890s.

AFRO-AMERICAN HISTORICAL SOCIETY OF DELAWARE
512 East 4th Street, Wilmington, DE 19801
(302) 655-7161
Mon-Fri 1-5.
Free.

Sponsors activities and exhibits relating to black history and culture.

DELAWARE MUSEUM OF NATURAL HISTORY
5 Miles Northwest of Wilmington on DE 52
Wilmington, DE
(302) 652-7600
Mon-Sat 9:30-4:30. Sun noon-5.
Adults $3.50. Seniors $2.50. Children $2.

Exhibits include information on the natural history
of African people.

District of Columbia

MARTIN LUTHER KING JR. MEMORIAL LIBRARY
901 G Street, NW, Washington, DC 20001
(202) 727-1285

Has a mural showing King's life and exhibits which detail
the history of the civil rights movement.

BETHUNE MUSEUM AND ARCHIVES
1318 Vermont Avenue NW, Washington, DC 20005
(202) 332-1233
Tues-Fri 10-4. Sun 12:30-4.
Free.

Five galleries within this fully restored nineteenth century
townhouse hold the photographs, manuscripts, paintings,
and artifacts covering the history and contributions of black
women to America and the world.

DECATUR HOUSE
748 Jackson Place NW, Washington, DC 20006
(202) 842-0920
Tours every half-hour, Tues-Fri 10-2. Weekends noon-4.
Adults $3. Seniors and ages 6-18 $1.50.

In the 1830s, John Gadsby, a hotel owner and nortorious slave trader, lived in the house. While Gadsby threw stylish balls in his drawing room, he kept slaves slated to be sold, in his attic where they could hear the music.

Georgia

THE ATLANTA LIFE INSURANCE HEADQUARTERS
100 Auburn Avenue NE, Atlanta, GA
Mon-Thurs. 8-4:30.
Free.

Atlanta Life, one of the largest black insurance companies in America, was founded in 1927 by Alonzo Herndon, a former slave.

MARTIN LUTHER KING, JR. CENTER
FOR NONVIOLENT SOCIAL CHANGE
449 Auburn Avenue, Atlanta, GA 30312
(404) 524-1956
Mon-Fri 9-5.
Free.

Houses manuscripts, records, audio visual material and oral histories of the civil rights movement from the 1950s and 1960s.

APEX (AFRICAN-AMERICAN PANORAMIC
EXPERIENCE) MUSEUM
135 Auburn Avenue NE, Atlanta, GA 30303
(404) 521-2739
Tues-Sat 10-5. Wed 10-6. Sun 1-5.
Adults $2. Children under 12 and seniors $1

Houses a collection of Afro-American life and heritage. Audio-visual presentations, art, artifacts and exhibits. There is a replica of the first black owned drug store in Georgia.

EBENEZER BAPTIST CHURCH
407 Auburn Avenue NE, Atlanta, GA

Martin Luther King was associate pastor of the church and preached from its pulpit. The church was the base from which the Southern Christian Leadership Conference spread through the South.

HERNDON HOUSE
587 University Place NW, Atlanta, GA 30350
(404) 993-8173
Tues-Sat 10-4.
Free.

The one time home of Alonzo Herndon, founder of the Atlanta Life Insurance Company. Home was built in 1910 and holds family treasures as well as oral histories of the Herndon family.

BIRTHPLACE OF DR. KING
501 Auburn Street, Atlanta, GA 30312
(404) 524-1956
Open daily 10-5 from June-August. 10-3:30 rest of the year.
Free. Guided tours are available.

THE HARRIET TUBMAN HISTORICAL AND CULTURAL MUSEUM
340 Walnut Street, Macon, GA 31208
(912) 743-8544
Mon-Fri 10-5. Weekends 2-6.
Free.

Aside from the section dedicated to Tubman, the museum also has exhibits which chronicle black achievements in different fields.

KING-TISDELL COTTAGE
514 East Huntingdon Street, Savannah, GA 31401
(912) 234-8000
Daily 12-5. Closed holidays. Adults $1.50.

Contains bills of sale for slaves written in Arabic by plantation slaves, African weapons, a dugout canoe, baskets, and carvings.

FIRST AFRICAN BAPTIST CHURCH
23 Montogmery Street, Savannah, GA
(912) 233-6597

The first Baptist church built of brick in North America. Holes in the floorboards are believed to be airholes for escaped Africans hidden by church members beneath the building.

Illinois

MUHAMMAD UNIVERSITY OF ISLAM
7351 South Stony Island, Chicago, IL 60649
(312) 643-0700
By appointment.

Headquarters run by the Nation of Islam which stresses belief in Allah as the true God and the separation of the black and white races.

SOUTHSIDE COMMUNITY ART CENTER
3831 S. Michigan Avenue, Chicago, IL 60653
(312) 373-1026
Mon-Fri 9-5. Weekends Noon-5. Closed holidays.
Adults $2. Seniors and students $1.

Opened in 1935, this gallery features works by black artists, primarily from the Chicago area and dating back to the 1940s.

DUSABLE MUSEUM OF AFRICAN-AMERICAN HISTORY
740 E. 56th Place, Chicago, IL 60637
(312) 947-0600
Mon-Fri 9-5. Weekends Noon-5. Closed holidays.
Adults $2. Seniors and students $1.

Historic and contemporary art collection from the 1940s through the 1960s with samples of African art such as wood carvings, drums, dolls, ancient spirit masks.

JOHNSON PUBLISHING COMPANY
820 S. Michigan Avenue, Chicago, IL 60605
(312) 322-9250
Tours by appointment.

Headquarters of *Ebony* and *Jet* magazines.

MALCOLM X COLLEGE
1900 West Van Buren, Chicago, IL 60612
(312) 942-3000
Open during regular school hours.
Free.

A junior college with an art gallery on campus displaying works of professional artists and students.

Indiana

CHILDREN'S MUSEUM
3000 N. Meridian Street (U.S. 31), Indianapolis, IN 46206
(317) 924-5431
Sat 10-5. Sun noon-5.
Adults $4. Seniors and children 2-17 $3.

Has a permanent exhibit area devoted to "African-American Scientists and Inventors from A to Z" featuring famous and not so widely known people.

MADAME WALKER URBAN LIFE CENTER
617 Indiana Avenue, Indianapolis, IN 46202
(317) 236-2099
Price varies with tour.

A restoration of the former headquarters for the cosmetic business of Madame C. J. Walker. The center provides meeting space for organizations. Displays on the life and work of Madame Walker, who was America's first black female millionaire. Tours of the center must be arranged two weeks in advance. Tours, which run between 8:30 and 5, may be combined with catered lunch or with Friday night "Jazz on the Avenue."

Louisiana

AMISTAD RESEARCH CENTER
Tilton Hall, Tulane University
6823 St. Charles Street, New Orleans, LA 70118
(504) 865-5000
Daily 8:30-5.
Free.

Documents on black-white relations ranging from the late 1700s to the present. Also contains 110 African art objects and 250 Afro-American art works.

THE FRENCH QUARTER
Bordered by Canal Street, Esplanade Avenue, Rampart Street, and the Mississippi River, New Orleans, LA

A living museum, the Quarter has about seven thousand residents and many hotels, guest houses, restaurants, museums, jazz clubs, quaint shops, expensive antique stores, and sleek shopping malls.

GRAVE OF MARIE LAVEAU, VOODOO QUEEN
North Claiborne Avenue and Bienville Street
St. Louis Cemetery Number 2, Square No. 3
New Orleans, LA
Visits to this cemetery are conducted by the National Park Service (504-589-2636).

Final resting place of a black woman who was famous in New Orleans in the 1800s for her "voodoo powers." The story is that she could heal the sick, cure the lovelorn, and put a hex on a person's enemies.

LOUIS ARMSTRONG PARK
North Rampart and St. Ann Street, New Orleans, LA

Slaves used to meet on Sundays in this park for traditional African song and dance. Today, it memorializes the great jazz musician. The statue of Armstrong is by black sculptor Elizabeth Catlett.

MARDI GRAS
New Orleans, LA

Held in February or March (count back forty-six days from Easter for exact date), this festival has been called "the greatest free show on earth." Extravagant floats, which are animated, illuminated, and loaded with masqueraders, roll throughout the city accompanied by Dixieland bands, high stepping marching bands, horsemen in plumed helmets, clowns, and torchbearers.

NEW ORLEANS HISTORIC VOODOO MUSEUM
724 Rue Dumaine, New Orleans, LA 70116
(504) 523-7685
Daily 10-6.
Adults $4. Seniors $3. Children $2.

Exhibits include African masks, carvings, instruments used in ritual music, and voodoo dolls. A more extensive tour includes visits to the bayous, plantations, Indian burial grounds, and a voodoo cemetery. Tours range from 2 1/2 to 10 hours.

Maryland

GREAT BLACKS IN WAX MUSEUM
1601 East North Avenue, Baltimore, MD 21213
(410) 563-3404
Tues-Sat 9-6. Sun 12-6. Closed Mondays except during February.
Adults $4.50. Seniors $4. Students 12-17 $3.

America's first black wax historic museum features more than one hundred life-size, lifelike wax figures of people like

Harriet Tubman, George Washington Carver, Rosa Parks, and Malcolm X. The displays are presented chronologically, highlighting ancient Africa, the Middle Passage, slavery, the Civil War, Reconstruction, the Harlem Renaissance, the civil rights movement, and the present.

BALTIMORE'S BLACK AMERICAN MUSEUM
1769 Carswell Street, Baltimore, MD 21218
(410) 243-9600
Mon-Thurs 9-5. Fri 7-11pm.
Free.

Exhibits artwork associated with the civil rights movement from the 1960s and 1970s.

CAB CALLOWAY JAZZ INSTITUTE
Parlett Moore Library, Coppin State College
2500 West North Avenue, Baltimore, MD 21216
(410) 383-5400
Mon-Fri 8-5.
Free.

Collection includes photos and memorabilia of jazz musician Cab Calloway.

EUBIE BLAKE NATIONAL MUSEUM
AND CULTURAL CENTER
409 N. Charles Street, Baltimore, MD 21201
(410) 396-1300
Tues-Fri 12-6. Weekends 12-5.
Free.

Has a panoramic display of Eubie Blake's life which includes musical scores, photos, paintings and correspondence of the composer who collaborated in more than one hundred songs.

NAACP NATIONAL HEADQUARTERS

26 West 25th Street, Baltimore, MD 21218
(410) 366-3300

Houses an archive which documents the organization's work over more than seventy years.

FREDERICK DOUGLASS MEMORIAL AND HISTORICAL ASSOCIATION

c/o Mary E. C. Gregory
10594 Twin Rivers Road, Apt. # E-1, Columbia, MD 21044
(301) 854-2938

Provides daily guided tours of the Frederick Douglass memorial home to inform visitors of how Douglass (1817-95) lived and of his contributions to the struggle for liberty, brotherhood, and citizenship.

Michigan

MOTOWN HISTORICAL MUSEUM

2648 W. Grand Boulevard, Detroit, MI 48208
(313) 875-2264
Tues-Sat 10-5. Sun 2-5. Other times by appointment.
Adults $3. Children under 12 $2.

Former Motown headquarters turned into a museum with unique photographs, vintage clothing, memorabilia and artifacts that conjure up the history of the Motown label.

MUSEUM OF AFRICAN-AMERICAN HISTORY

Detroit Cultural Center
301 Frederick Douglass Street, Detroit, MI 48202
(313) 833-9800
Wed-Sat 9:30-5.
All tours free, but donations are welcome.

Founded in 1965, the museum's goals are to produce programs that raise black self esteem and recover lost black heroes. Has exhibits depicting scenes from traditional Africa, the history of Michigan's underground railroad, and famous slave revolts. Black Music Month is celebrated each June.

NATIONAL MUSEUM OF THE TUSKEGEE AIRMEN
6325 W. Jefferson Avenue, Detroit, MI 48202
(313) 297-9360
By appointment only.

This museum tells the story of the first black pilots to take to the air during World War II. They were dubbed the "Black Birdmen" by the Germans, who had both fear and admiration for them.

New York

ABYSSINIAN BAPTIST CHURCH
132 West 138th Street, New York, NY 10030
(212) 862-7474

One of the oldest black churches in the country was started by eighteen black worshippers who split away from the white First Baptist Church on Gold Street in lower Manhattan. Abyssinian has always served as a public forum for religious, social, and political concerns of blacks. Has an exhibit devoted to Adam Clayton Powell, Jr.'s, career in the church.

AFRO ARTS CULTURAL CENTER
2192 Adam Clayton Powell, Jr. Boulevard
New York, NY 10027
(212) 996-3333
Daily 9-5.
Donation.

This is a combination cultural/educational facility which presents performances along with an African museum.

APOLLO THEATER
253 West 125th Street, New York, NY 10027
(212) 749-5838

In the 1930s the Apollo Theater began presenting variety shows featuring leading black entertainers.

AUNT LEN'S DOLL AND TOY MUSEUM
6 Hamilton Terrace, New York, NY
(212) 281-4143
Tours by appointment only.

Houses more than ten thousand black and multi-ethnic dolls from around the world.

BLACK FASHION MUSEUM
157 West 126th Street, New York, NY
(212) 666-1320
Mon-Fri 1-8.
Adults $1.00. Children under 12, fifty cents.

Did you know that a black fashion designer created Jackie Kennedy's wedding gown for her highly publicized marriage to JFK? The wedding gown is on display here along with other memorabilia of black fashion including books, photographs, textiles, clothing, jewelry, oral history, and tapes.

CENTER FOR AFRICAN ART
593 Broadway, New York, NY 10012
(212) 966-1313
Tues-Fri 10-5. Sat 11-5. Sun 12-5.
Adults $2.50. Students/seniors/children $1.50.

Housed in two restored townhouses, the museum focuses on the richness and variety of African culture.

FRAUNCES TAVERN

54 Pearl Street, New York, NY 10004
(212) 425-1778
Mon-Fri 10-4. Adults $2.50. Seniors and under 12 $1.

It was at the black owned Fraunces Tavern that General George Washington said farewell to the officers of the Continental Army in 1783. Today, there is still a restaurant on the first floor. A museum about the tavern's history and the Revolutionary War occupies the upper floors.

MALCOLM SHABAZZ MASJID (MOSQUE OF ISLAM)

130 West 113th Street, New York, NY 10025
(212) 662-4100

The four storied mosque is the East Coast headquarters for the Muslim faith. It is named in honor of Malcolm X.

SCHOMBERG CENTER FOR RESEARCH IN BLACK CULTURE

515 Lenox Avenue, New York, NY 10037
(212) 491-2214
Mon-Wed 12-8. Thurs-Sat 10-6.
Free.

Started in 1926 by Arthur Schomburg, this has become the most important center in the world for the study of black people. The Schomberg Center has materials ranging from rare items from the earliest African kingdoms to contemporary civil rights materials, books, magazines, photographs, manuscripts, and playbills that document the black experience.

STUDIO MUSEUM IN HARLEM
144 West 125th Strteet, New York, NY 10027
(212) 864-4500
Wed-Fri 10-5. Sat and Sun 1-6.
Adults $2. Seniors/students/children $1.

A collection of paintings, photography and folk art by
African-American artists. The museum conducts a variety
of workshops, concerts, film programs and organizes
traveling exhibits.

North Carolina

NORTH CAROLINA MUSEUM OF HISTORY
109 East Jones Street, Raleigh, NC 27601
(919) 733-3894
Tues-Sat 9-5. Sun 1-6. Closed major holidays.
Free.

This museum has the only collection of work by Thomas
Day, a highly skilled nineteenth century furniture designer
who owned his own factory and trained black and white
carpenters.

Ohio

CINCINNATI MUSEUM OF NATURAL HISTORY
17209 Gilbert Avenue, Cincinnati, OH 45203
(513) 287-7000
Tues-Sat 9-5. Sun noon-5.
Closed holidays. Adults $3. Under 12 $1.

Has special exhibits and programs on African art and culture.

AFRICAN-AMERICAN MUSEUM
1765 Crawford Road, Cleveland, OH 44106
(216) 791-1700
Mon-Thurs 12-3. Fri 12-8. Sat Noon-3.
Adults $2. Children $1.

Features books, speeches, paintings, photographs, and tapes
that celebrate the black church, black music, and African-
American achievers.

CLEVELAND MUSEUM OF ART
1150 East Boulevard, Cleveland, OH 44106
(216) 421-7340
Tues-Fri 10-5:45. Wed 5:45-9:45. Sat 9-4:45. Sun 1-5:45.
Closed holidays. Free.

Has a good African art selection.

HARRIET TUBMAN MUSEUM
9250 Miles Park, Cleveland, OH
(216) 341-1202
Tues-Thurs by appointment. Sat and Sun 1-4.
Adults $3. Children $2.

Named after one of the greatest women in American history,
this museum has records and artifacts that chronicle the life
of Harriet Tubman, who helped hundreds of blacks escape
from slavery. Also has an exhibit dedicated to Garrett
Morgan, the black native of Cleveland who invented the
gas mask and electric traffic light.

Oklahoma

NATIONAL COWBOY HALL OF FAME
AND WESTERN HERITAGE CENTER
1700 NE 63rd Street, Oklahoma City, OK 73111
(405) 478-2250
Daily 8:30-6.
Adults $4. Senior citizens $3. 6-12 $1.50.

A memorial to the men and women who pioneered the West
including a tribute to famed black rodeo rider, Bill Pickett,
who originated a style called bulldogging which got him
elected to the National Cowboy Hall of Fame.

Pennsylvania

AFRO-AMERICAN HISTORICAL
AND CULTURAL MUSEUM
7th and Arch Streets, Philadelphia, PA
Tues-Sat 10-5. Sun 1-6. Closed Monday and major holidays.
Adults $3.50. Under 13 and over 61 $1.75.

A historical and art museum, the facility depicts African-
American culture from colonial times to the present.

ALL WARS MEMORIAL TO BLACK SOLDIERS
West Lansdowne Drive, Fairmount Park, Philadelphia, PA

A statue erected in 1934 to honor black soldiers from
Pennsylvania who had fought in America's wars.

South Carolina

BOONE HALL PLANTATION
9 miles north of Charleston on U.S. 17,
Charleston, SC 29465
(803) 884-4371
Mon-Sat 8:30-6:30. Sun 1-5.
Adults $6. Seniors $5. Ages 6-12 $2.

One of the largest cotton plantations in the south before the
Civil War, Boone Hall covered 17,000 acres and used more
than a thousand slaves. Today, sections of the plantation,
including the mansion and slave quarters, are open to the
public.

CABBAGE ROW
89-91 Church Street, Charleston, SC

The street was the inspiration for Catfish Row in George
Gershwin's *Porgy and Bess*. The row of tenements got the
nickname from the vegetables residents offered for sale on
their windowsills.

DENMARK VESEY HOUSE
56 Bull Street, Charleston, SC

The former home of a free black Charleston carpenter who,
in 1822, recruited dozens of black city workers and organized
a large scale slave revolt.

SULLIVAN'S ISLAND
U.S. Route 17 or 703

Located across the harbor from Charleston's Fort Sumter, the island was the entry point for nearly 40 percent of all Africans bought to this country during the 1800s. The island is also the site of the Old Slave Mart Library, a multi-media collection of material.

Tennessee

BEALE STREET HISTORICAL TOUR (3 Hours).
Memphis, TN
Call Heritage Tours (901) 527-3427.

Tour includes the home of W. C. Handy known as "the father of the blues," First Baptist Beale Street Church, which was built by slaves with handmade bricks, and the Memphis Music and Blues Museum.

NATIONAL CIVIL RIGHTS MUSEUM
450 Mulberry Street, Memphis, TN 38103
(901) 521-9699

Freedom Summer is a permanent exhibit which captures the struggle of African-Americans who, against white opposition, exercised their right to vote in the 1950s.

Virginia

MAGGIE L. WALKER NATIONAL HISTORIC SITE
110 1/2 East Leigh Street, Richmond VA 23219
(804) 780-1380
Wed-Sun 9-5.
Free.

Restored former home of Maggie L. Walker. Walker was black, female, and disabled. Nevertheless, she was the first American woman to start a bank in the United States. She also ran an insurance company and edited a newspaper.

6

Professional Associations

It is always a good career move to network in your chosen field. The following directory can get you started but try to avoid wasting time, money, and energy by joining the wrong associations. Before signing up, make sure you have figured out your career goals and what you expect to gain from membership. Visit at least two meetings or events sponsored by the group and ask questions like:

What type of service and support do members receive?

What events are scheduled for the next three to six months?

What opportunities exist for members to take on leadership roles?

If the organizations' goals and style match your own, then it is to your benefit to get involved and meet other professionals in your field.

AFRICAN HERITAGE STUDIES ASSOCIATION

c/o Africana Studies and Research Institute
Queens College, Flushing, NY 11367
(718) 520-7416
Founded: 1969

Composed of persons of African descent absorbed in the research and teaching of African history. Purposes are to reconstruct and present African history and cultural studies in a way that is pertinent to African people.

AFRICAN STUDIES ASSOCIATION

c/o Dr. Edna Bay
Credit Union Building, Emory Building, Atlanta, GA 30322
(404) 329-6410
Founded: 1957   Members: 2,200

For teachers, writers, and researchers of Africa including political scientists, historians, geographers, anthropologists, economists, librarians, and linguists.

AFRO-AMERICAN POLICE LEAGUE

P.O. Box 49122, Chicago, IL 60649
(312) 753-9454
Founded: 1968   Members: 2,500

For African-American police officers. Seeks to enhance the relationship between citizens of the black community and police departments; improve the relationship between black policemen and white policemen; and educate the public about police departments.

AFRO-AMERICAN POLICE OFFICERS LEAGUE
4101 San Jacinto, Houston TX 77027
(713) 522-2850

The League seeks to represent both the concerns of black police officers as well as the minority community of Harris County.

AMERICAN ASSOCIATION OF BLACKS IN ENERGY
1220 L Street NW Suite 605, Washington, DC 20005
(202) 898-0828
Founded: 1977   Members: 500

Blacks in energy-related professions; including engineers, scientists, consultants, academians, and entrepreneurs. Aspires to expand the awareness of the minority community in energy issues.

AMERICAN BLACK CHIROPRACTORS ASSOCIATION
1918 East Grand Boulevard, St. Louis, MO 63107
(314) 531-0615

The group represents the concerns of its members and offers career information, counseling, and possible scholarship aid to encourage black students to enter the field.

ARIZONA COUNCIL OF BLACK ENGINEERS AND SCIENTISTS
P.O. Box 27082, Tempe, AZ 85282

A group which seeks to meet the needs of its members and to encourage young minority group members to enter the field.

ASSOCIATION OF AFRICAN-AMERICAN WOMEN ENTREPRENEURS

814 Thayer Avenue Suite 202, Silver Spring, MD 20910
(301) 565-0527
Founded: 1983   Members: 1,500

Seeks to assist in developing a greater number of successful self employed black women through business and personal development programs, networking, and legislative action.

ASSOCIATION OF BLACK ADMISSION AND FINANCIAL AID OFFICERS OF THE IVY LEAGUE AND SISTERS

P.O. Box 1019, Astor Station, Boston, MA 02123
(413) 538-2023
Aims to improve upon the means of recruitment, selection, financial aid packaging, and support services designed to boost and preserve the minority student population.

ASSOCIATION OF BLACK CPA FIRMS

1101 Connecticut Avenue NW, Washington, DC 20036
(202) 857-1100

Wishes to raise the status of black CPA firms as well as support their activities.

ASSOCIATION OF BLACK PERSONNEL IN CITY GOVERNMENT

5462 Crenshaw Boulevard, Los Angeles, CA 90043
(213) 290-3070

This group was formed to help give black government employees more of a voice in determining policies and conditions which affect them.

ATLANTA BLACK NURSES ASSOCIATION

4450 Creek Valley Court, SW, Atlanta, GA 30331
(404) 344-6779

This is a regional association involved with enhancing health services available to minorities and with improving the professional status of its members.

BLACK BUSINESS ALLIANCE

2713 Classen Avenue, Baltimore, MD 21215
Founded: 1979   Members: 250

Acts as a national and international support system for black businesses, providing assistance in organizational management and resource development.

BLACK DATA PROCESSING ASSOCIATES

P.O. Box 7466, Philadelphia, PA 19101
(215) 925-0811
Founded: 1976

Unites black data-processing workers for career advancement. Sponsors educational programs and works to bring more minorities into the field.

BLACK ENTERTAINMENT AND SPORTS LAWYERS ASSOCIATION

111 East Wacker Drive #600, Chicago, IL 60601
(212) 586-6130
Founded: 1979

Lawyers representing black clients in the fields of entertainment and sports. Goal is to work on matters of mutual concern and to help insure that clients are not handicapped by restrictive policies or inappropriate representation.

BLACK NURSES ASSOCIATION OF SAN DIEGO
P.O. Box 14269, San Diego, CA 92114

Promotes professional growth, recruits, counsels, and assists those in or considering nursing.

BLACK PHOTOGRAPHERS OF CALIFORNIA
107 Santa Barbara Plaza, Los Angeles, CA 90008
(213) 294-9024

This organization was formed to provide for exchange of information among black photographers. It also provides a support and networking system to encourage black photographers.

BLACKS IN LAW ENFORCEMENT
256 East McLemore Avenue, Memphis, TN 38106
(901) 774-1118
Founded: 1986   Members: 500
Seeks to educate the public concerning the contributions made by blacks in the field of law enforcement. Records the lives and accomplishments of the first blacks to participate in law enforcement in the United States. Publications: *Blacks In Law Enforcement/Quarterly*.

BLACK STUNTMEN'S ASSOCIATION
8949 West 24th Street , Los Angeles, CA 90034
(213) 870-9020
Founded: 1966   Members: 34

Serves as an agency for stunt people in motion pictures and television. Conducts stunt performances at various local schools. Maintains library of TV and motion picture films.

BLACK TENNIS FOUNDATION

1893 Amsterdam Avenue, New York, NY 10032
(212) 926-5991

Among its other activities, the foundation helps African-American youths acquire skills and begin a career in this field.

BLACK WOMEN IN PUBLISHING

P.O. Box 6275, F.D.R. Station, New York, NY 10150
(212) 772-5951
Founded: 1979

A networking and support group that expedites the exchange of ideas and information among members, especially regarding career planning and job security. Sponsors lectures, panel discussions, seminars, workshops, and other programs on topics such as computers in publishing, freelance journalism, and images of black women in literature.

BLACK WORLD FOUNDATION

P.O. Box 7106, San Francisco, CA 94120
(415) 541-0311
Seeks to encourage and support the development of black writers and black cultural and political thought.

CONGRESSIONAL BLACK ASSOCIATES

P.O. Box 23793, L'Enfant Plaza Station S.W.
Washington, DC 20026
(202) 225-4288
Founded: 1979

Black congressional staff members. Provides information on the operation of the federal government to members and the black community; fosters contacts among members and the community.

DISTRICT OF COLUMBIA BLACK WRITER'S WORKSHOP

615 Kensington Place, NE, Washington, DC 20011
(202) 832-8932

This is an organization of black playwrights and is concerned with the development of black writers and black-related drama.

INTERNATIONAL BLACK WRITERS

4019 South Vicennes Avenue, Chicago, IL 60653
(312) 995-5195
Founded: 1970

Founded by black authors, this organization wants to encourage black writers to publish more works exhibiting black beliefs after the civil rights movement of the 1960s.

MINORITY PHOTOGRAPHERS

67 East 4th Street, New York, NY 10003
(212) 673-1021

This organization offers training sessions and exhibit opportunities to help minorities trying to enter the field of commercial photography.

NATIONAL ASSOCIATION OF BLACK ACCOUNTANTS (NABA)

900 Second Street NE Suite 205, Washington, DC 20002
(202) 682-0222
Founded: 1969   Members: 3,000

For CPAs, accountants, and accounting students. To unite accountants and accounting students who have similar interests and ideals, who are committed to professional and academic excellence, who possess a sense of professional and civic responsibility and who are concerned with advancing opportunities for minorities in the accounting profession. Programs include: free income tax preparation, student scholarships, high school and university career seminars, regional student conferences, technical seminars and lectures. Maintains speakers bureau and placement service.

NATIONAL ASSOCIATION OF BLACKS IN CRIMINAL JUSTICE

P.O. Box 66271, Washington, DC 20035
(202) 686-2961
Founded: 1972   Members: 5,000

Criminal justice professionals concerned with the impact of criminal justice policies and practices on the minority community.

NATIONAL ASSOCIATION OF BLACK GEOLOGISTS AND GEOPHYSICISTS

P.O. Box 720157, Houston, TX 77272
Founded: 1981   Members: 120

Assists minority geologists and geophysicists in establishing professional and business relationships.

NATIONAL ASSOCIATION OF BLACK HOSPITALITY PROFESSIONALS

P.O. Box 5443, Plainfield, NJ 07060
(201) 354-5117
Founded: 1985   Members: 50

For individuals involved in the hospitality profession on a managerial or supervisory level and those interested in careers in the field. Its purposes are to provide a forum for the sharing of ideas, experiences, and job opportunity information.

NATIONAL ASSOCIATION OF BLACK JOURNALISTS

P.O. Box 17212, Washington, D.C. 20041
(703) 648-1270
Founded: 1975   Members: 2,000

Aims are to strengthen the ties between blacks in the black
media and blacks in the white media; sensitize the white
media to the "institutional racism in its coverage."
Works with high schools to identify potential journalists.

NATIONAL ASSOCIATION OF BLACK LAW ENFORCEMENT EXECUTIVES

908 Pennsylvania Avenue SE, Washington, DC 20003
(202) 546-8811
Founded: 1976

For law enforcement executives above the rank of lieutenant,
police educators, academy directors. Goals are to provide a
platform on which the concerns and opinions of minority law
enforcement executives and command level officers can be
expressed.

NATIONAL ASSOCIATION OF BLACK OWNED BROADCASTERS

1730 M Street NW Rm 412, Washington, DC 20036
(202) 463-8970
Founded: 1976   Members: 150

Represents the interests of existing and potential black radio
and television stations. Is currently working with the Office
of Federal Procurement Policy to ascertain which major
advertisers and advertising agencies are following government
suggestions to increase the amount of advertising dollars
received by companies owned by African-Americans.

NATIONAL ASSOCIATION OF BLACK SOCIAL WORKERS

271 West 125th Street, Room 317, New York, NY 10027
(212) 348-0035
Founded: 1968 Members: 10,000

Seeks to support, develop, and sponsor community welfare projects and programs which will serve the interest of the black community and aid it in controlling its social institutions.

NATIONAL ASSOCIATION OF BLACK WOMEN ATTORNEYS

3711 Macomb Street NW; Second Floor,
Washington, DC 20016
(202) 966-9693
Founded: 1972 Members: 500

For black women who are members of the bar of any U.S. state or territory; associate members include law school graduates, paralegals and law students. Seeks to: advance jurisprudence and the administration of justice by increasing the opportunities of black and non-black women at all levels.

NATIONAL ASSOCIATION OF BLACK WOMEN ENTREPRENEURS

P.O. Box 1375, Detroit, MI 48231
(313) 341-7400
Founded: 1979 Members: 3,000

Objective is to enhance business, professional, and technical development of both present and future black businesswomen.

NATIONAL BLACK MCDONALD'S OPERATORS ASSOCIATION
5434 King Avenue, No. 3, Pennsauken, NJ 08110
(609) 662-2030
Founded: 1972   Members: 169

For Black owners of McDonald's restaurants. Provides a forum for the exchange of ideas on the improvement of community relations and on the operation and management of restaurants.

NATIONAL COALITION OF BLACK MEETING PLANNERS
50 F Street NW Suite 1040, Washington, DC 20001
(202) 628-3952
Founded: 1983   Members: 400

Intentions are to act as intermediary between hotels, airlines, convention centers and bureaus in an effort to measure the impact of minorities in these fields.

NATIONAL CONSORTIUM FOR BLACK PROFESSIONAL DEVELOPMENT
2210 Goldsmith Office Center, Suite 228-A,
Louisville, KY 40218
Founded: 1974
(502) 451-8199   Members: 57

Goal is to increase substantially, by the year 2000 the number of black professionals in business administration, communications, applied and natural sciences, engineering and law. Sponsors a science and engineering competition for black students and Ph.D. programs in the agricultural sciences and business administration. Provides recruitment service for universities seeking qualified black faculty and students.

ORGANIZATION OF BLACK AIRLINE PILOTS

P.O. Box 86, La Guardia Airport, New York, NY 11371
(201) 568-8145
Founded: 1976   Members: 650

Cockpit crew members of commercial air carriers, corporate pilots, and other interested individuals. Seeks to increase minority involvement in the aerospace industry.

YOUNG BLACK PROGRAMMERS COALITION

P.O. Box 11243, Jackson, MS 39213
(601) 634-5775
Founded: 1976   Members: 2,615

Provides professional and technical assistance to black entrepreneurs in the broadcast and music industries.

CHAPTER

7

Videotapes

Black film history did not begin with Eddie Murphy in *Beverly Hills Cop* or even with Richard Roundtree as the black leather-clad private eye in *Shaft*. Blacks have been on the screen ever since moving pictures were invented. During the silent era (from the turn of the century until 1929), the important black parts were given to white actors who played the roles in blackface. The real black actors were used in supporting roles or as extras. This practice stopped in 1929 with the advent of the "talkies," but, unfortunately, Hollywood's portrayal of blacks on screen did not get any better. The majority of films created and released by the major Hollywood studios from 1930 until today show blacks, as famed historian Donald Bogle says, "either as gentle Toms, doomed mulattoes, comic coons, mammies, whores, substance abusers, or mean/violent black bucks."

No amount of pressure would force the Hollywood chieftains to reverse their position so black independent filmmakers stepped into the picture in the 1930s and started creating their own reels. These early films were called race movies because they were geared to reach the mass black audience. Because the early productions were poorly financed and the producers lacked training, some of the race movies were technically awful, but the black audiences of the 1930s eagerly paid to see them because the characters were always professional people, not maids, butlers, or bootblacks.

The most prolific and flamboyant of these early black filmmakers was Oscar Micheaux (1884-1951). Born in Illinois, Micheaux worked as a pullman car porter and as a farmer before deciding to become a filmmaker. Although the lighting and editing in Micheaux's films were dreadful, the themes were sound, and blacks were portrayed as three dimensional characters. Micheaux created a stable of black performers and off-camera personnel modeled after the Hollywood studio system. He developed a loyal following and was a first rate film publicist and promoter. Oscar Micheaux is an important name in black history because he proved that there was a market for black cinema and that a black star system could exist.

Micheaux's films include *The Homesteader* (1919); *The Brute* (1920); *Symbol of the Unconquered* (1920); *Jasper Landry's Will* (1923); *The Spider's Web* (1926); *The Millionaire* (1927); *Wages of Sin* (1929); *Ten Minutes To Kill* (1933); *Harlem After Midnight* (1934); *Lem Hawkin's Confession* (1935); *Swing* (1938); *Lying Lips* (1939) and *The Notorious Elinor Lee* (1940).

After 1940 and Oscar Micheaux, nothing much changed in the world of independent black filmmaking. And then Melvin

Van Peebles came along in the early 1970s with *Sweet Sweetback's Baadasssss Song*. In an interview with *Newsweek* about the film, Van Peebles said: "All the films about black people up to now have been told through the eyes of the Anglo-Saxon majority—in their rhythms and speech and pace. They've been diluted to suit the white majority just like Chinese restaurants tone down the spices to suit American tastes. I want white people to approach *Sweetback* the way they do an Italian or Japanese film. They have to understand *our* culture. In my film, the black audience finally gets a chance to see some of their fantasies acted out—about rising out of the mud and kicking ass." Just as he predicted, black audiences loved *Sweetback* and the mainstream press attacked the film for its radical political vision, sex and graphic violence. *The New York Times* said: "Instead of dramatizing injustice, Van Peebles merchandises it." Huey Newton called *Sweetback* "a revolutionary masterpiece."

It took a lot of nerve for Melvin Van Peebles to defy tradition by refusing to make a sentimental "things can work out between white and black" movie. His bravery paved the way for dozens of black films featuring radicalized black heroes out to assert themselves and at odds with the system.

And then Spike Lee came along with *She's Gotta Have It*, a hilarious film with characters that are relaxed and comfortable in their blackness. The film was also unique because it was the first slice-of-life comedy created with realistic black situations and dialogue delivered without obvious concern for mainstream understanding or acceptance. Lee became an instant hero in the black community and over the next few years frequently quarreled with Hollywood honchos for complete control over his films and their messages. In his quest for reel power, Lee released important films like *School Daze*, *Do The Right Thing*, and *Jungle Fever*.

Spike Lee and black America finally triumphed with his masterpiece, *Malcolm X*. In order to do justice to Malcolm X's life and vision, Lee's production went millions of dollars over budget, and he needed still more money to complete it. Warner Brothers stopped the filming and refused to give him additional funding to complete the project. Spike Lee turned to the black community for help and received at least $1 million from Oprah Winfrey, Bill Cosby, Prince, Tracy Chapman, and Janet Jackson. *Malcolm X* opened on schedule to rave reviews and, most importantly, lifted Malcolm to the heroic position that he has long deserved.

That was reel power.

The following videos were originally motion picture releases either aimed at black audiences or with an African-American playing a significant role and are available for rent at your local video store. If you have trouble locating any of these tapes, please contact Beverly DeBase, Alternate Video, 837 Exposition Avenue, Dallas, TX 75226 (214) 823-6030. Her store deals exclusively in these products and she should be able to help.

ACROSS 110TH STREET (1972)
102 minutes, rated R
Yaphet Kotto, Paul Benjamin, Ed Bernard, Anthony Quinn, Antonio Fargas. Three black men disguised as cops steal $300,000 from a bank that is controlled by the mob. The son-in-law of the head mobster tries to catch the bandits before the police do to teach them a lesson ... gangland style.

ACTION JACKSON (1988)
95 minutes, rated R
Carl Weathers, Vanity, Bill Duke, Craig T. Nelson. A dedicated police officer tries to save a beautiful woman from a gangster's grip in this action packed drama.

ANGEL HEART (1987)
113 minutes, rated R
Mickey Rourke, Robert De Niro, Lisa Bonet. De Niro hires a small time detective to find a missing man. A steamy sex scene was snipped by seconds to avoid an X-rating in the U.S. It is restored in the video version.

ANOTHER 48 HOURS (1990)
95 minutes, rated R
Nick Nolte, Eddie Murphy. This sequel to *48 Hours* has Murphy on the hit list of two men who are determined to catch him. Nolte steps in and helps save Murphy's life.

AUTOBIOGRAPHY OF MISS JANE PITTMAN (1974)
110 minutes, rated PG
Cicely Tyson, Odetta, Thalmus Rasulala. Tyson is at her best in the role of Miss Jane Pittman, a 110 year old ex-slave who tells her life story from the Civil War to the beginning of the civil rights movement.

BEVERLY HILLS COP (1984)
105 minutes, rated R
Eddie Murphy, Judge Reinhold, Lisa Eilbacher, Stephen Elliott, Paul Reiser, Damon Wayans. Murphy is a wise-cracking Detroit cop who arrives in Beverly Hills to find the people who killed his best friend. This tough and very funny role was originally created for Sylvester Stallone.

BEVERLY HILLS COP II (1987)

102 minutes, rated R

Eddie Murphy, Judge Reinhold, Brigitte Nielsen. Murphy goes back to Beverly Hills because his friend, police captain Ronny Cox has been critically wounded by a ring of thugs.

BILL COSBY "HIMSELF" (1982)

105 minutes, rated PG

Cosby tickles the funny bone with stories about raising children, human nature, and family life.

THE BINGO LONG TRAVELING ALL-STARS AND MOTOR KINGS (1976)

110 minutes, rated PG

Billy Dee Williams, James Earl Jones, Richard Pryor. Bright, original comedy set in 1939 about a baseball player trying to buck the system by starting his own team.

BIRD (1988)

161 minutes, rated PG

Forest Whitaker. Biography of jazz great Charlie Parker who was considered to be the greatest saxophonist of all time.

BLACK CAESAR (1973)

96 minutes, rated R

Fred Williamson, Larry Cohen, Gloria Hendry. A hard core gangster film with Fred Williamson shooting and clawing his way to the top of the crime world.

BLACK EYE (1974)

98 minutes, rated PG

Fred Williamson, Rosemary Forsyth, Richard Anderson, Teresa Graves. Mystery with a black private eye investigating the murders which surround a drug ring in California.

BLACK GIRL (1972)
97 minutes, rated PG
Ossie Davis, Brock Peters, Leslie Uggams, Claudia McNeil, Louise Stubbs, Gloria Edwards, Ruby Dee. An aspiring dancer and her two half-sisters are ruthless in trying to obtain a better life.

BLACK GUNN (1972)
98 minutes, rated R
Jim Brown, Martin Laundau, Brenda Sykes. A black nightclub owner goes after the whites who were behind the murder of his brother.

BLACK LIKE ME (1964)
107 minutes, rated PG
Carl Lerner, James Whitmore, Roscoe Lee Browne, Al Freeman, Jr., Raymond St. Jacques. Based on the true story of a white reporter who took drugs so that he could pass for black and experience racial prejudice firsthand.

BLACK MAMA, WHITE MAMA (1972)
87 minutes, rated R
Pam Grier, Margaret Markov, Sid Haig, Lynn Borden. Violent remake of The Defiant Ones. Markov and Grier are convicts who escape from a Filipino prison camp.

BLACULA (1972)
92 minutes, rated PG
Denise Nicholas, Vonetta McGee, Thalmus Rasulala, Ketty Lester. The story goes like this: Dracula bit a black prince and he turned into a vampire to stalk the streets of Los Angeles.

BLAZING SADDLES (1974)
93 minutes,, rated R
Cleavon Little, Gene Wilder. Richard Pryor was one of the
writers of this scathing spoof of the Wild Wild West featuring Little as a black sheriff sent to clean up a rowdy town.

BLUE COLLAR (1978)
114 minutes,, rated R
Richard Pryor, Yaphet Kotto. Drama about auto workers who
rise up against their coroprate bosses and their own union.

BOOMERANG (1992)
118 minutes, rated R
Eddie Murphy, Halle Berry, Robin Givens, David Alan Grier,
Martin Lawrence, Grace Jones, Geoffrey Holder, Eartha
Kitt, Chris Rock, Tisha Campbell, John Witherspoon,
Melvin Van Peebles. A playboy meets his match, gets his
heart broken, and learns lessons about friendship and true
love.

BOSS NIGGER (1975)
92 minutes, rated PG
Fred Williamson, D'Urville Martin, R. G. Armstrong,
William Smith, Barbara Leigh. A Western with Williamson
as a bounty hunter who always gets his man.

BOYZ N THE HOOD (1991)
107 minutes, rated R
Larry Fishburne, Ice Cube, Cuba Gooding, Jr., Nia Long,
Morris Chestnut, Tyra Ferrell, Angela Bassett, Whitman
Mayo. A divorced father strives to raise his son with values
and black pride under trying circumstances in South Central
Los Angeles.

BREWSTER'S MILLIONS (1985)
97 minutes, rated PG
Richard Pryor, John Candy, Lonette McKee, Tovah
Feldshuh, Hume Cronyn. Richard Pryor as a man who must
spend $30 million in one month in order to inherit the grand
sum of $300 million.

BROTHER FROM ANOTHER PLANET (1984)
104 minutes, rated R
Joe Morton, Darryl Edwards, Steve James, Rosette Le Noire,
David Strathairn. A black visitor from another plant who
lands in Harlem impresses most people he meets because he
lets them do all the talking and doesn't say anything.

CABIN IN THE SKY (1943)
100 minutes
Eddie "Rochester" Anderson, Lena Horne, Ethel Waters,
Louis Armstrong, Rex Ingram, Duke Ellington and His
Orchestra. Lena Horne is a temptress who lures hapless
Eddie "Rochester" Anderson away from Ethel Waters.

CARBON COPY (1981)
92 minutes, rated PG
Denzel Washington, George Segal, Susan Saint James, Paul
Winfield. A white businessman is shocked into confronting
his stereotypical views when he learns that he has a black
teenaged son.

CARMEN JONES (1954)
105 minutes
Dorothy Dandridge, Harry Belafonte, Pearl Bailey, Roy
Glenn, Diahann Carroll, Brock Peters. A factory worker falls
in love with a G.I. who is engaged to be married, leading to
tragedy.

CLASS ACT (1992)

100 minutes rated PG-13

Christopher (Kid) Reid, Christopher (Play) Martin. A genius with a perfect SAT score finds his scholastic records switched with a teenaged convict. The thug forces him to go along with the error.

CLARA'S HEART (1988)

108 minutes, rated PG-13

Whoopi Goldberg, Michael Ontkean, Kathleen Quinlan, Neil Patrick Harris, Spalding Gray, Beverly Todd. Goldberg plays a West Indian maid who works for a rich young white couple and counsels their vulnerable little boy.

CLAUDINE (1974)

92 minutes, rated PG

Diahann Carroll, James Earl Jones, Lawrence Hilton-Jacobs, Tamu, Adam Wade. Love story about a welfare mother of six who falls in love with a sanitation man who wants her but can't deal with the system she is caught up in.

CLEOPATRA JONES (1973)

89 minutes, rated PG

Tamara Dobson, Bernie Casey, Shelley Winters, Brenda Sykes, Antonio Fargas, Bill McKinney, Esther Rolle. A government agent who is also a karate expert goes after drug lords.

CLEOPATRA JONES AND THE CASINO OF GOLD (1975)

96 minutes, rated R

Tamara Dobson, Stella Stevens, Norman Fell, Caro Kenyatta. Wild, woolly, sexy, violent sequel to Cleopatra Jones.

THE COLOR PURPLE (1985)
152 minutes, rated PG-13
Danny Glover, Whoopi Goldberg, Margaret Avery, Oprah Winfrey, Willard Pugh, Akosua Busia, Desreta Jackson, Adolph Caesar, Rae Dawn Chong, Dana Ivey, Larry Fishburne. The story of abused black girl who is forced into a bad marriage against her will and searches for happiness over the next three decades.

COME BACK CHARLESTON BLUE (1972)
100 minutes, rated PG
Raymond St. Jacques, Godfrey Cambridge, Jonelle Allen, Adam Wade, Peter DeAnda. A sequel to *Cotton Comes to Harlem* finds police officers Coffin Ed and Gravedigger Jones trying to keep law and order in Harlem amidst some colorful characters.

COMING TO AMERICA (1988)
116 minutes, rated R
Eddie Murphy, Arsenio Hall, James Earl Jones, John Amos, Madge Sinclair, Shari Headley. Murphy is an African prince who wants to choose his own wife and decides that he will find her in Queens, New York. John Amos is excellent as the prospective bride's gold digging father.

COOL BREEZE (1972)
101 minutes, rated R
Thalmus Rasulala, Judy Pace, Jim Watkins, Lincoln Kilpatrick, Sam Laws, Margaret Avery, Raymond St. Jacques. Proceeds of a diamond robbery are earmarked to set up a black people's bank if the bandits don't go to jail first.

COOLEY HIGH (1975)
107 minutes, rated PG
Glynn Turman, Lawrence Hilton-Jacobs, Garrett Morris, Cynthia Davis, Corin Rogers, Maurice Leon Havis. A coming-of-age film set in Chicago 1964 where a simple joy ride results in a tragic misunderstanding.

CORNBREAD, EARL AND ME (1975)
95 minutes, rated PG
Moses Gunn, Bernie Casey, Rosalind Cash, Madge Sinclair, Keith Wilkes, Tierre Turner. A black teen gets accepted into college on a basketball scholarship but is gunned down by police bullets before he can accept it.

THE COTTON CLUB (1984)
127 minutes, rated R
Richard Gere, Gregory Hines, Diane Lane, Lonette McKee, Bob Hoskins, James Remar, Nicolas Cage, Allen Garfield, Fred Gwynne, Gwen Verdon, Maurice Hines, Larry Fishburne. Colorful gangsters and an old fashioned Duke Ellington soundtrack surround this crime tale set in the world famous nightclub.

COTTON COMES TO HARLEM (1970)
97 minutes, rated R

Godfrey Cambridge, Raymond St. Jacques, Calvin Lockhart, Judy Pace, Redd Foxx, Emily Yancy, Cleavon Little. St. Jacques is Coffin Ed Johnson, Cambridge is Gravedigger Jones, two black cops who suspect that a preacher's back to Africa campaign is a scam.

CRY FREEDOM (1987)
157 minutes, rated PG
Kevin Kline, Penelope Wilton, Denzel Washington, John Thaw, Timothy West, Zakes Mokae. A black South African activist strikes up a friendship with a white, crusading newspaper editor.

DAUGHTERS OF THE DUST (1991)
114 minutes, rated PG
Cora Lee Day, Alva Rodgers, Adisa Anderson, Kaycee Moore, Barbara O, Eartha D. Robinson, Bahni Turpin, Cheryl Lynn Bruce. Poetic story of the Gullah people who are descendants of the slaves who settled on islands near South Carolina and Georgia.

D.C. CAB (1983)
99 minutes, rated R
Irene Cara, Anne DeSalvo, Max Gail, Gloria Gifford, DeWayne Jessie, Bill Maher, Whitman Mayo, Mr. T, Paul Rodriguez, Gary Busey, Marsha Warfield. Comedy about a run down Washington taxi company staffed by a group of weirdos who straighten up when times get hard.

DEF BY TEMPTATION (1990)
95 minutes
Cynthia Bond, Kadeem Hardison, Bill Nunn, Melba Moore, Samuel Jackson. Students at a Christian school visit a friend in New York City and get involved with a seductress.

DOLEMITE (1975)
88 minutes, rated R
Rudy Ray Moore, Jerry Jones, Lady Reed. Comic Rudy Ray Moore tells stories about life, love and the ladies.

DO THE RIGHT THING (1989)

120 minutes, rated R

Danny Aiello, Ossie Davis, Ruby Dee, Richard Edson, Spike Lee, Giancarlo Esposito, Joie Lee, Bill Nunn, John Turturro, Paul Benjamin, John Savage. A white pizza parlor owner staunchly refuses to put pictures of African-American heroes on the wall in the black community where his business is located. The police arrive to ward off violence and cause tragedy instead.

THE EDUCATION OF SONNY CARSON (1974)

105 minutes, rated R

Rony Clanton, Don Gordon, Joyce Walker, Paul Benjamin, Ram John Holder. Based on Carson's autobiography, this is a drama about teens in Brooklyn during the late fifties and early sixties.

FAME (1980)

134 minutes, rated R

Irene Cara, Lee Curreri, Eddie Barth, Laura Dean, Paul McCrane, Barry Miller, Gene Anthony Ray, Maureen Teefy, Antonio Franceschi, Anne Meara, Albert Hague. Students at New York City's High School of Performing Arts sing and dance up a storm to take a shot at stardom and deal with personal problems at the same time.

THE FIVE HEARTBEATS (1991)

122 minutes, rated R

Robert Townsend. Musical drama about the rise and fall of a black singing group who battle the drug addiction of one member, racism from music industry honchos, and their own overnight success back in the 1960s.

48 HOURS (1982)
97 minutes, rated R
Nick Nolte, Eddie Murphy, Annette O'Toole, James Remar, Frank McRae, David Patrick Kelly, Sonny Landham, Brion James, Olivia Brown, The Busboys. A tired cop gets a convict out of jail for two days to help him catch a cop killer. The Busboys soundtrack is a real treat.

GHOST DAD (1990)
84 minutes, rated PG
Bill Cosby, Kimberly Russell, Denise Nicholas, Ian Bannen, Christine Ebersole, Barry Corbin, Salim Grant, Brooke Fontaine, Dakin Matthews, Dana Ashbrook, Arnold Stang. Cosby is a single father who dies in a taxi accident and, as a ghost, tries to make his three kids financially secure.

GLORY (1989)
122 minutes, rated R
Matthew Broderick, Denzel Washington, Cary Elwes, Morgan Freeman, Jihmi Kennedy, Andre Braugher, John Finn, Donovan Leitch, John David Cullum, Bob Gunton. America's first unit of black soldiers during the Civil War experience racism at the hands of the government they are fighting and dying to protect.

THE GOLDEN CHILD (1986)
96 minutes, rated PG-13
Eddie Murphy, Charlotte Lewis, Charles Dance, Victor Wong, Randall "Tex" Cobb, James Hong, J. L. Reate. A "perfect " child is kidnapped and Murphy is the only who can save him.

THE GREAT WHITE HOPE (1970)
101 minutes, rated PG
James Earl Jones. Story of turn-of-the-century boxer
Jack Johnson facing challenges in and out of the ring.

THE HARDER THEY COME (1973)
98 minutes, rated R
Jimmy Cliff. A drug dealer kills a cop in a drug bust
and becomes a folk hero. Great soundtrack.

HARLEM NIGHTS (1989)
115 minutes, rated R
Eddie Murphy, Richard Pryor, Redd Foxx, Danny Aiello,
Michael Lerner, Della Reese, Berlinda Tolbert, Stan Shaw,
Jasmine Guy, Arsenio Hall, Robin Harris. The owner of
an after-hours spot in 1930s Harlem (Pryor) and his adopted
son (Murphy) stand up to a white mobster who wants to close
the club.

HEART CONDITION (1990)
98 minutes, rated R
Denzel Washington, Bob Hoskins. A man who recently died
returns to earth after his heart is transplanted into another
man's body. The two of them form a team to track down the
drug lords who killed him.

HELL UP IN HARLEM (1973)
96 minutes, rated R
Fred Williamson, Julius W. Harris, Gloria Hendry,
Margaret Avery. Sequel to *Black Caesar* features Williamson
who tries to clean up New York City and kills anyone who
tries to stop him.

A HERO AIN'T NOTHIN' BUT A SANDWICH (1978)

105 minutes, rated PG

Cicely Tyson, Paul Winfield, Larry B. Scott, Helen Martin, Glynn Turman, David Groh. Based on Alice Childress' book an intelligent teenager who gets into drugs.

HOLLYWOOD SHUFFLE (1987)

82 minutes, rated R

Robert Townsend, Anne-Marie Johnson, Starletta Dupois, Helen Martin, Craigus R. Johnson, Keenan Ivory Wayans, Steve James. A young black actor tries to make it in Hollywood but gets frustrated by the stereotypical roles that are constantly thrust at him.

HOUSE PARTY (1990)

100 minutes, rated R

Christopher "Kid" Reid, Robin Harris, Christopher "Play" Martin, Martin Lawrence, Tisha Campbell, A. J. Johnson, Paul Anthony. Hilarious comedy about black middle class teenagers trying to have a good old fashioned house party who run into problems with parents, hoodlums, and the police.

HOUSE PARTY 2 (1991)

94 minutes, rated R

George Jackson, Christopher "Kid" Reid, Christopher "Play" Martin, Eugene Allen, George Anthony Bell, Georg Stanford Brown, Tony Burton, Tisha Campbell, Iman, Kamron, Queen Latifah, Martin Lawrence, Helen Martin, William Schallert. Sequel to *House Party* shows Kid entering college but having problems holding on to the money that his church has raised for his education.

HOW TO MAKE LOVE TO A NEGRO WITHOUT GETTING TIRED (1989)

97 minutes, rated R

Isaach de Bankole, Maka Kotto, Antoine Durand, Jacques Legras, Roberta Bizeau, Miriam Cyr. A black Haitian writer lives in Montreal and takes advantage of racial stereotypes to bed wealthy white girls.

IDENTITY CRISIS (1990)

98 minutes, rated R

Mario Van Peebles, Ilan Mitchell-Smith, Nicholas Kepros, Shelley Burch, Rick Aviles, Melvin Van Peebles, Olivia Brown, Bobby Rivers. The spirit of a white fashion designer is somehow transferred into the body of a black rapper.

I'M GONNA GIT YOU SUCKA (1988)

87 minutes, rated R

Keenan Ivory Wayans, Bernie Casey, Antonio Fargas, Steve James, Isaac Hayes, Jim Brown, Ja'net DuBois, Dawnn Lewis, John Vernon, Clu Gulager, Kadeem Hardison, Damon Wayans, Anne Marie Johnson, Gary Owens, Eve Plumb, Clarence Williams III, David Alan Grier, Kim Wayans, Robin Harris, Chris Rock. Hilarious spoof of seventies blaxploitation films with hero Jack Spade setting out to avenge the death of his brother.

IMITATION OF LIFE (1959)

124 minutes

Lana Turner, John Gavin, Sandra Dee, Dan O'Herlihy, Susan Kohner, Robert Alda, Juanita Moore, Mahalia Jackson, Troy Donahue, Jack Weston. A tearjerker focusing on two single mothers raising daughters alone in the 1950s.

IN THE HEAT OF THE NIGHT (1967)
109 minutes
Sidney Poitier, Rod Steiger, Warren Oates, Lee Grant, Scott Wilson, Larry Gates, Quentin Dean, James Patterson, Anthony James, William Schallert. Virgil Tibbs is a visitor in a small Southern town when the police chief asks him to help investigate the murder of a wealthy factory owner.

THE JACKIE ROBINSON STORY (1950)
76 minutes
Ruby Dee, Minor Watson, Louise Beavers, Richard Lane, Harry Shannon, Ben Lessy, Joel Fluellen. Biography of Robinson, the first black man to play major league baseball.

JO JO DANCER, YOUR LIFE IS CALLING (1986)
97 minutes, rated R
Richard Pryor, Debbie Allen, Art Evans, Fay Hauser, Barbara Williams, Carmen McRae, Paula Kelly, Diahnne Abbott, Scoey Mitchell, Billy Eckstine, Wings Hauser, Virginia Capers. Pryor examines his early life and his first show business encounters.

THE JOSEPHINE BAKER STORY (1991)
130 minutes, rated R
Lynn Whitfield, Ruben Blades, David Dukes, Louis Gossett, Jr., Craig T. Nelson, Kene Holliday, Vivian Bonnell. Rags to riches to rags story of the black girl from St. Louis who became an international superstar.

JUICE (1992)
92 minutes, rated R
Omar Epps, Jermaine Hopkins, Tupac Shakur, Khalil Kain, Cindy Herron, Vincent Laresca, Samuel L. Jackson. Four black teenagers rob a liquor store with tragic consequences.

JUMPIN' JACK FLASH (1986)

100 minutes, rated R
Whoopi Goldberg, Stephen Collins, John Wood,
Carol Kane, Annie Potts, Peter Michael Goetz, Roscoe Lee
Browne, Sara Botsford, Jerome Krabbe, Jonathan Pryce,
Jon Lovitz, Phil Hartman, Tracy Reiner, Jim Belushi,
Paxton Whitehead, Tracey Ullman, Jamey Sheridan.
Whoopi Goldberg plays a computer operator who gets
into international intrigue trying to help a British spy.

JUNGLE FEVER (1991)

132 minutes, rated R
Spike Lee, Wesley Snipes, Annabella Sciorra, Ossie Davis,
Ruby Dee, Samuel L. Jackson, Lonette McKee,
John Turturro, Frank Vincent, Anthony Quinn, Halle Berry,
Tyra Ferrell, Veronica Webb. A married black architect gets
into a disatrous love affair with his white secretary.

KRUSH GROOVE (1985)

97 minutes, rated R
Blair Underwood, Joseph Simmons, Sheila E., The Fat Boys,
Daryll McDaniels, Kurtis Blow. Rap musical biography that
tells the story of Russell Simmons and the start of Def Jam
Records.

LADY SINGS THE BLUES (1972)

144 minutes, rated R
Diana Ross, Billy Dee Williams, Richard Pryor, James
Callahan, Paul Hampton, Sid Melton. Diana Ross plays
Billie Holiday in this story of the jazz singer's life.

THE LAST DRAGON (1985)
109 minutes, rated PG
Taimak, Vanity, Chris Murney, Julius J Carry 3rd,
Keshia Knight Pulliam. A martial arts expert falls in love
with a glamorous video deejay and risks his life to save her
from a crook.

LEAN ON ME (1989)
104 minutes, rated R
Morgan Freeman. A high school principal takes control of a
school overrun by drugs, violence, and apathy. By ignoring
city rules, he makes the students want to learn, saves a few
lives, and boosts the overall reading scores.

THE LEARNING TREE (1969)
107 minutes, rated R
Autobiography of Gordon Parks who grew in rural 1920s
Kansas.

LET'S DO IT AGAIN (1975)
112 minutes, rated PG
Sidney Poitier, Bill Cosby, Jimmie Walker, Calvin Lockhart,
John Amos, Denise Nicholas, Lee Chamberlain. Hilarious
follow-up to *Uptown Saturday Night*. Lodge brothers Poitier
and Cosby hypnotize Jimmie Walker into becoming a great
boxer.

LILIES OF THE FIELD (1963)
95 minutes
Sidney Poitier, Lilia Skalia. When Poitier's car breaks down
in front of a convent, the German nuns decide he has been
sent by God to repair their ramshackle building. Poitier
received an Oscar for his engaging performance.

LIVIN' LARGE (1991)
96 minutes, rated R
Terence "TC" Carson, Lisa Arrindell, Blanche Baker, Nathaniel "Afrika" Hall, Julia Campbell, Bernie McInerney, Loretta Devine. A young man gets a chance to be a television newsman and finds out that money and fame don't mean everything.

THE MACK (1973)
110 minute, rated R
Max Julien, Don Gordon, Richard Pryor, Carol Speed, Roger E. Mosley, William C. Watson. A black pimp in Oakland makes lots of money managing a group of prostitutes until he discovers the error of his ways.

MANDINGO (1975)
126 minutes, rated R
James Mason, Susan George, Perry King, Richard Ward, Brenda Sykes. Tale about a black sexual superstud set on a pre-Civil War plantation.

MAHOGANY (1975)
109 minutes, rated PG
Diana Ross, Billy Dee Williams, Anthony Perkins, Jean-Pierre Aumont, Beah Richards, Nina Foch. A fashion designer becomes world famous and is unhappy without her true love back home.

MALCOLM X (1992)

201 minutes, rated R

Denzel Washington, Spike Lee, Angela Bassett, Albert Hall, Al Freeman Jr., Delroy Lindo. Spectacular biography of the late Malcolm X from his childhood in Nebraska to his life as a muslim and champion of the black cause. Interesting note: The film does not reveal that Farrakhan was Malcolm X's protege or that the two men enjoyed a close personal friendship for many years until Malcolm's bitter feud with the muslims divided them.

MANDELA (1987)

135 minutes, rated R

Danny Glover, Alfre Woodard. The story of the jailed anti-apartheid activist whose lifelong battle against the injustice in his country served as a rallying cry around the world.

THE MIGHTY QUINN (1989)

95 minutes, rated R

Denzel Washington, Robert Townsend. An entertaining evening of mystery with Denzel Washington in the role of Xavier Quinn, a police chief on a small Caribbean island investigating the death of a white businesman.

MO' BETTER BLUES (1990)

127 minutes, rated R

Denzel Washington, Spike Lee, Wesley Snipes, Giancarlo Esposito, Robin Harris, Joie Lee, Bill Nunn, Dick Anthony Williams, Cynda Williams, Ruben Blades, Abbey Lincoln. A self centered jazz musician juggles women and stands by his friend/manager until his career is destroyed.

NATIVE SON (1986)

112 minutes, rated R

Victor Love, Oprah Winfrey. The story of a poor black youth living in 1930s Chicago who accidentally kills a rich, white girl and is sentenced to death.

NEW JACK CITY (1991)

97 minutes, rated R

Wesley Snipes, Ice T, Allen Payne, Chris Rock, Mario Van Peebles, Judd Nelson, Michael Michele, Bill Nunn, Russell Wong, Vanessa Williams, Nick Ashford, Thalmus Rasulala. Two maverick ex cops set out to bring down a millionaire crack dealer.

PENITENTIARY (1979)

99 minutes, rated R

Leon Isaac Kennedy, Thommy Pollard, Badja Djola, Hazel Spears, Gloria Delaney, Chuck Mitchell. A convict has problems in prison until his talent as a boxer comes to light.

PIECE OF THE ACTION (1977)

135 minutes, rated PG

Sidney Poitier, Bill Cosby, James Earl Jones, Denise Nicholas, Hope Clark, Tracy Reed, Titos Vandis, Ja'net DuBois. Con men find themselves obligated to help a social worker get slum kids on the right track.

PINKY (1949)

102 minutes

Jeanne Crain, Ethel Barrymore, Ethel Waters, Nina Mae McKinney, William Lundigan. A black girl who routinely passes for white returns to her southern roots.

PRINCESSE TAM-TAM (1935)
77 minutes
Josephine Baker, Albert Prejean, Robert Arnoux, Germaine Aussey, Georges Peclet, Viviane Romance, Jean Galland. A poor, beautiful African girl is polished by a writer and then passed off as an Indian princess.

PURLIE VICTORIOUS (1963)
105 minutes
Ossie Davis, Ruby Dee, Godfrey Cambridge. Film version of Ossie Davis' Broadway satire about a free wheeling preacher who goes up against an oppressive, bigoted landowner.

PURPLE RAIN (1984)
111 minutes, rated R
Prince, Apollonia Kotero, Morris Day, Olga Karlatos, Clarence Williams III, Jerome Benton, Billy Sparks. Prince's film debut as a young musician who struggles to gain acceptance and help his battered mother.

A RAGE IN HARLEM (1991)
108 minutes, rated R
Forest Whitaker, Gregory Hines, Robin Givens, Danny Glover, Zakes Mokae, Badja Djola, John Toles-Bey, Ron Taylor, Stack Pierce, George Wallace, Willard E. Pugh, Samm-Art Williams, Tyler Collins, Screamin Jay Hawkins. A beautiful woman from Mississippi arrives in Harlem to sell a load of gold and gets involved with a mama's boy who falls in love with her.

A RAISIN IN THE SUN (1961)
A black family looks for a way out of the Chicago ghetto. Sidney Poiter is the middle aged son who realizes he is trapped for life unless he can find a way out soon.

THE RETURN OF SUPERFLY (1990)
95 minutes, rated R
Nathan Purdee, Margaret Avery, Leonard Thomas, Christopher Curry, David Groh. Sequel to *Superfly* with Nathan Purdee replacing Ron O'Neal as Priest except he isn't into drugs anymore and tries to stop his former pals who are.

RICHARD PRYOR HERE AND NOW (1983)
83 minutes, rated R
Concert film made months after his near fatal accident, Pryor jokes about sobriety and success plus sex and race.

RICOCHET (1991)
97 minutes, rated R
Denzel Washington, John Lithgow, Ice T, Kevin Pollak, Lindsay Wagner, Mary Ellen Trainor, Josh Evans, Victoria Dillard, John Amos, John Cothran, Jr. A street cop becomes a hero when he gets a vicious killer locked up, but the madman plots revenge.

SCHOOL DAZE (1988)
114 minutes, rated R
Spike Lee, Larry Fishburne, Giancarlo Esposito, Tisha Campbell, Kymee, Joe Seneca, Art Evans, Ellen Holly, Ossie Davis, Branford Marsalis, Kadeem Hardison, Darryl M. Bell, Joie Lee, Jasmine Guy, Gregg Burge, Kasi Lemmons, Phyllis Hyman. Life on a black college campus in the South where a student activist fights against the administration while other students try to get into fraternity life or fight each other over color.

SCREAM BLACULA SCREAM! (1973)
95 minutes, rated PG
William Marshall, Don Mitchell, Pam Grier,
Michael Conrad, Richard Lawson. Sequel to *Blacula* shows
the vampire rising from eternal rest and biting necks in the
black community.

SHAFT (1971)
100 minutes, rated R
Richard Roundtree, Moses Gunn, Charles Cioffi,
Christopher St. John, Drew Bundini Brown, Gwenn
Mitchell, Lawrence Pressman, Antonio Fargas. A sexy, black
private eye named John Shaft is hired by a gangster to find a
terrified young girl who has been kidnapped by the mob.

SHAFT'S BIG SCORE (1972)
104 minutes, rated R
Richard Roundtree, Moses Gunn, Drew Bundini Brown,
Joseph Mascolo, Kathy Imrie, Wally Taylor, Joe Santos.
Sequel to *Shaft* has private eye Roundtree against the mob
again as he investigates a friend's murder.

SHAFT IN AFRICA (1973)
112 minutes, rated R
Richard Roundtree, Frank Finlay, Vonetta McGee, Neda
Arneric, Cy Grant, Jacques Marin. Shaft helps an African
nation stop latter-day slave trading.

SHE'S GOTTA HAVE IT (1986)

100 minutes, rated R
Tracy Camilla Johns, Spike Lee, Redmond Hicks,
John Canada Terrell, Raye Dowell. Nola Darling is a happy,
beautiful and sexy graphic designer. The problem with Nola's
men is that there are three of them and they don't want to
share her. The problem with Nola is that there is only one of
her—and she wants all three.

SILVER STREAK (1976)

113 minutes, rated PG
Richard Pryor, Gene Wilder, Jill Clayburgh, Patrick
McGoohan, Ned Beatty, Richard Kiel, Scatman Crothers.
Pryor and Wilder outwit gangsters while riding a supertrain
from Los Angeles to Chicago.

A SOLDIER'S STORY (1984)

101 minutes, rated PG
Howard E. Rollins, Adolph Caesar, Dennis Lipscomb, Art
Evans, Denzel Washington, Larry Riley, David Alan Grier,
Robert Townsend, Patti LaBelle, Wings Hauser, Trey
Wilson. Howard Rollins plays Captain Davenport, a black
lawyer sent from Washington to investigate the murder of
Sergeant Waters, a black officer at a southern military post.

SOUL TO SOUL (1971)

95 minutes, rated G
Wilson Pickett, Ike and Tina Turner, Santana, Roberta Flack,
Les McCann, Willie Bobo, Eddie Harris, the Staple Singers.
Documentary of soul, jazz, and gospel performances in
concert

SOUNDER (1972)
105 minutes, rated G
Cicely Tyson, Paul Winfield, Kevin Hooks, Carmen Mathews, Taj Mahal, James Best, Janet MacLachlan. Experiences of a black sharecropping family in the 1930s.

SPARKLE (1976)
98 minutes, rated PG
Philip Michael Thomas, Irene Cara, Lonette McKee, Dwan Smith, Dorian Harewood, Mary Alice. Three sisters start a singing group and try to break into show business.

STORMY WEATHER (1943)
77 minutes
Lena Horne, Bill "Bojangles" Robinson, Cab Calloway, Katherine Dunham, Fats Waller, Dooley Wilson, the Nicholas Brothers. Bill Bojangles and Lena Horne are a couple in this classic musical romance.

SUPERFLY (1972)
96 minutes, rated R
Ron O'Neal, Carl Lee, Sheila Frazier, Julius W. Harris, Charles McGregor. A Harlem drug dealer tries for one big score before he quits the business. ✓

SUPERFLY T.N.T. (1973)
87 minutes, rated R
Ron O'Neal, Roscoe Lee Browne, Sheila Frazier, Robert Guillaume, Jacques Sernas, William Berger, Roy Bosier. Black ex drug pusher decides to help an official from an African country. ✓

SWEET SWEETBACK'S BAADASSS SONG (1971)

97 minutes, rated R

Melvin Van Peebles, Rhetta Hughes, Simon Chuckster, John Amos. Until he sees two white cops savagely beat a young black revolutionary, a black pimp called Sweetback has pursued a life of pleasure without thinking about anything else. After seeing the beating, Sweetback hacks up the two white cops and becomes a fugitive trying to reach the Canadian border. A classic.

TAP (1989)

110 minutes, rated PG-13

Gregory Hines, Suzzanne Douglas, Sammy Davis, Jr. Savion Glover, Joe Morton, Dick Anthony Williams, Terrence McNally, Sandman Sims, Bunny Briggs, Steve Condos, Jimmy Slyde, Pat Rico, Arthur Duncan, Harold Nicholas, Etta James. A man who shunned his tap dancing heritage finds that the call of tap is just too strong and goes back to dancing.

THANK GOD IT'S FRIDAY (1978)

90 minutes, rated PG

Donna Summer, Valerie Landsburg, Terri Nunn, Chick Vennera, Ray Vitte, Jeff Goldblum, Paul Jabara, Debra Winger, Andrea Howard, The Commodores. One night in the life a disco focuses on carefree dance and the search for romance.

THEY CALL ME MISTER TIBBS! (1970)

108 minutes, rated PG

Sidney Poitier, Barbara McNair, Martin Landau, David Sheiner, Anthony Zerbe, Jeff Corey, Ed Asner. Detective Tibbs is now married and living in San Francisco where he is assigned to track down another murderer.

T.N.T. JACKSON (1974)
73 minutes, rated R
Jeanne Bell, Stan Shaw, Pat Anderson, Ken Metcalf.
A karate expert searches for her missing brother.

THE TOY (1982)
99 Minutes, rated PG
Richard Pryor, Jackie Gleason, Scott Schwartz, Teresa
Ganzel, Ned Beatty, Wilfrid Hyde-White, Annazette Chase.
Pryor is a penniless writer hired by zillionaire Gleason as
plaything for spoiled son Schwartz.

TRADING PLACES (1983)
106 minutes, rated R
Eddie Murphy, Dan Aykroyd, Jamie Lee Curtis, Ralph
Bellamy, Don Ameche, Denholm Elliott. A comedy in which
the wiles of a street smart black man, an uptight broker,
a white hooker and an English butler outwit two society
millionaires who think they can play God with people's lives.

UNDER THE CHERRY MOON (1986)
98 minutes, rated PG-13
Prince, Jerome Benton, Kristin Scott-Thomas, Steven
Berkoff, Francesca Annis, Emmanuelle Sallet, Alexandra
Stewart, Victor Spinetti. Prince is an American gigolo/
entertainer in the south of France who has women falling
at his feet.

UPTOWN SATURDAY NIGHT (1974)
104 minutes, rated PG
Sidney Poitier, Bill Cosby, Harry Belafonte, Calvin Lockhart,
Flip Wilson, Richard Pryor, Rosalind Cash, Roscoe Lee
Browne, Paula Kelly. Two pals try to retrieve a stolen winning
lottery ticket and get involved with a gangster.

WATERMELON MAN (1970)

97 minutes, rated R

Godfrey Cambridge, Estelle Parsons, Howard Caine, D'Urville Martin, Kay Kimberly, Mantan Moreland, Erin Moran. A prejudiced white man suddenly turns black and sees his life in a different way.

WHITE MEN CAN'T JUMP (1992)

114 minutes, rated R

Wesley Snipes, Woody Harrelson, Rosie Perez, Tyra Ferrell, Cylk Cozart, Kadeem Hardison, Ernest Harden, Jr. Two basketball hustlers take advantage of stereotypes to make money while trying to hold on to their women.

THE WOMEN OF BREWSTER PLACE (1989)

200 minutes, rated R

Oprah Winfrey, Mary Alice, Olivia Cole, Robin Givens, Moses Gunn, Jackee, Paul Kelly, Lonette McKee, Paul Winfield, Cicely Tyson. A film based on Gloria Naylor's novel spans several decades in the lives of seven black women who live in a tenement on a walled off street.

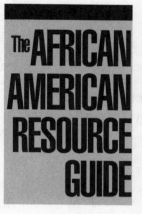

The AFRICAN AMERICAN RESOURCE GUIDE

Further Reading

There are a number of handbooks, encyclopedias, directories, and dictionaries in the reference room of your local library. These volumes are generally not available in bookstores and cannot be removed from the library. They mostly deal with statistical and general information about the black experience. Here is a partial list of the many reference books available.

TITLE	LIBRARY CALL NUMBER
A HARD ROAD TO GLORY: A HISTORY OF THE AFRICAN-AMERICAN ATHLETE A 3 volume set: Vol I: 1619-1918, Vol II: 1919-1945, Vol III: Since 1946	796.0899
BLACK AFRICA: **A COMPARATIVE HANDBOOK** Studies for the political, economic and social analysis of 41 Sub-Saharan countries.	967
BLACKS IN AMERICAN FILMS AND TELEVISION Award winning encyclopedia of films and television shows with information on writers, directors and major stars.	791.4308
BLACK AMERICANS INFORMATION DIRECTORY Sourcebook of information on nonprofit, private, public governmental agencies.	973.0496
BLACK LITERATURE CRITICISM Compilation of criticism about works by 125 black authors	809.8896
THE BLACK RESOURCE GUIDE National directory which includes business and health statistics	973.0496

TITLE	LIBRARY CALL NUMBER
CHRONOLOGY OF AFRICAN-AMERICAN HISTORY A chronological overview of the people, places and events that have had a major impact on African-American life from the 1600s to the present.	973.0496
CULTURAL ATLAS OF AFRICAN-AMERICANS Visual and narrative overview of black people, heritage and culture.	973.0496
DICTIONARY OF AFRO-AMERICAN SLAVERY A one volume encyclopedia	305.567
DIRECTORY OF AFRICAN-AMERICAN RELIGIOUS BODIES Historical overviews and bibliographies on African-American religious traditions.	280.0899
THE HARLEM RENAISSANCE: A HISTORICAL DICTIONARY FOR THE ERA This work of nearly eight hundred entries contains a wide range of information about the people and events of the period.	700.8996
HISTORIC LANDMARKS OF BLACK AMERICA A guide to over 300 sites significant to African-American history	917.3049

TITLE	LIBRARY CALL NUMBER
THE NEGRO ALMANAC: A REFERENCE WORK ON THE AFRICAN-AMERICAN Considered by many to be the definitive reference on the history and culture of African-Americans.	973.0496
THE STATE OF BLACK AMERICA Essays by scholars on a variety of critical issues.	305.896
THE STATE OF BLACK PHILADELPHIA Reports social indicators of the city's black population. Each volume focuses on a key issue, such as the state of children and youth.	305.896
STATISTICAL RECORD OF BLACK AMERICA A compilation of statistics in 19 subject categories	305.896

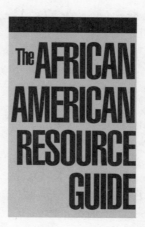

Bibliography

Cassidy, David. *The Graduate Scholarship Book*. 2d. ed.
Prentice Hall, 1990.

Elley, Derek. *Variety Movie Guide*.
Prentice Hall, 1992.

✓ *HBO's Guide To Movies on Video Cassette and Cable TV*.
HarperPerennial, 1991.

Kael, Pauline. *500l Nights at the Movies*.
Henry Holt, 199l.

Low, W. Augustus and Clift, Virgil A.
Encyclopedia of Black America.
Da Capo Press, 1981.

Maltin, Leonard. *Leonard Maltin's TV Movies and Video Guide*. Signet, 1992.

Scheuer, Steven H. *The Complete Guide to Videocassette Movies*. Henry Holt & Co., 1987.

Schlachter, Gail Ann. *Director of Financial Aids for Women*. Reference Service Press, 1991.

Schlacter, Gail Ann and Weber, R. David. *Directory of Finanical Aids for Minorities 1993-1995*. Reference Service Press, 1991.

Thum, Marcella. *Hippocrene USA Guide To Black America*. Hippocrene Books, 1991.

Walker, John. *Halliwell's Film Guide*. HarperCollins, 1991.